ONE LONG DAY

a book by Marshall Reeves

ONE LONG DAY

THE SEEDS ARE SOWN

RAAM is an affliction not unlike Poison Ivy. It gets under your skin, and although there may be no indications on the surface, the poison is still there, waiting to erupt. It is an itch that can be scratched, but the relief is temporary. The only cure is to finish the race. You can do any number of endurance bike races to calm the beast, but that is only a temporary treatment. Like Poison Ivy, the symptoms may be hidden, but the affliction is still there.

RAAM is the ultimate bicycle race challenge. Longer than any of the three "Grand Tours", it is the Holy Grail of endurance cycling. A 3000 mile non stop coast to coast race from California to Maryland, with strict time cutoffs along the way, as well as at the end. This stringent requirement has resulted in barely over 300 official "finishers" in its 35 year history, and only 10 over the age of 60. In contrast, the Holy Grail of mountaineering is Mt. Everest, and there have been over 5000 successful summits. In triathlon, it's the Ironman, and thousands have accomplished that. To finish RAAM, the solo racer must ride over 250 miles a day for 12 consecutive days. Since the clock doesn't stop, this means very little sleep. Usually no more than three hours a night.

I became infected in 2004 during an annual event called the "Cross Florida Ride". It was an event I had participated in several times before, but this year I was having trouble finding support. The ride is a point to point bicycle ride of 165 miles, starting in Cocoa Beach, Florida on the east coast, and finishing (at the time) on Pine Island, on the west coast. It is supported by the organizers, but in order to stay with the front group, personal ride support is required, as well as a ride home. Two offers fell through, but I was determined (stubborn), so decided to ride it unsupported. The plan was to carry enough supplies to make it across, then turn around and ride back as far as I could that day, get a hotel if needed, and finish the following day. Great plan!

The ride started at first light, and I soon realized how much differently a bicycle handles when you have twenty pounds on your back. The pace is always fast at the beginning, and this year was no exception, but it was Florida flat, so the extra weight was no factor. As usual, the 200 strong pack whittled down after about 40 miles, and a lead group of about 20 riders formed. It was the cast of usual characters. Among them was Rob Kish, someone I knew of, but didn't really know. When he asked why I was carrying the load, I explained, and he graciously offered me a ride back with him and his wife, Brenda. I should never have accepted that ride. We both finished near the front, then loaded into his van for the ride home. It was during that ride that the seeds of RAAM were sown. I knew he was a RAAM legend, but didn't realize he had entered 20 times, finished 18, and won three, while setting many records along the way. As we talked, I realized that RAAM was something I had to do.

By the time I decided to enter RAAM for the first time in 2011, I was no stranger to endurance events. I had completed about 100 triathlons, including 11 ironman length races (2.4 mile swim, followed by a 112 mile bike leg, and finishing with a 26.2 mile run). I had also competed in several 12 hour mountain bike events, and four 24 hour mountain bike races (twice world age group champion). Additionally, I raced a European version of RAAM called "Le Tour Ultime" on a two person team with the aforementioned Rob Kish. It was a great race starting and finishing in Holland that included many of the mountain climbs often seen in the Tour De France. We won that event, and it filled me with overconfidence.

Preparations for RAAM are daunting. The logistics alone are overwhelming. There's the crew, the equipment, travel, vehicles, getting time off, and of course coming up with the money. It is not a cheap race. The solo entry alone is several thousand dollars. Add to that the cost of food, travel, and lodging for the crew, vehicle expenses, and gear, and it could easily cost thirty thousand dollars. I'm sure the international racers spend even more. As daunting as it is for the racers, it is even more daunting for the race organizers. They must procure venues at the start and the finish, assemble a team of on course race officials, coordinate all the time stations, some manned, and some unmanned, go over the course immediately prior to the start of the race to make sure there are no last minute construction issues, and measure each turn to the tenth of a mile to be published in the official route book. Additionally, each crew receives several copies of the "GEAR" book. It is the tome sized document that explains race procedures, schedules, and rules.

RAAM has several categories in addition to "solo". There are two person teams, four person teams, and even eight person teams. There are also divisions within each category. These divisions are broken down by age group, gender, and type of bike ridden. The race has huge international appeal, and is, in fact, more well known in other countries where bicycle racing is more popular. As a result, there are usually more international entries than domestic. RAAM covers a prescribed route from Oceanside, California, to Annapolis, Maryland. There are time stations at approximately every 50 miles along the way. As the racer passes each time station, his crew must call that time in to race headquarters. The route covers 12 states, and traverses every type of terrain that exists in the United States. It crosses the Sierras, Rockies, Ozarks, and finally the Appalachians, resulting in over 175000 feet of climbing. Between the desert and the high Rockies, the temperatures can range from 115 degrees to 30 degrees. Three full days are spent at over 6000 feet of elevation. With those extremes, and the requirement of being on a bicycle for 20 plus hours a day, or 250-300 miles for as many as 12 consecutive days, it is no wonder that physical issues are the demise of many racers. This is why, in the 35 or so years of RAAM, so few people have ever completed the race in the allotted time.

Obstacles to a successful race are numerous. A few notable ones are nutrition, fatigue, altitude edema, cramps, saddle sores, numb hands and feet, crashes, crew mutiny, and in extreme cases, "Shermer's Neck", named for one of the original racers who suffered from it. It is a condition brought on by total failure of the neck muscles, making it impossible to hold one's head up. The only way to continue is by use of a cradle fabricated from rope and PVC. However, perhaps the greatest obstacle in this race is sleep deprivation. During my attempts at RAAM, I have experienced three distinct versions of sleeping on a bike. The most obvious was just flat out falling asleep, and waking up due to the sensation of falling. I never crashed as a result, but came awfully close. The second was like sleepwalking where I would lose track of time. I would look at my computer and have no recollection of the last 20 miles. The third, and most prevalent version was the dreamlike state. This was even more pronounced with the accumulation of sleep deprivation. This would be when hallucinations could occur. I never really hallucinated, but I sure did dream! All of that is worth it, however, because if you enter, you get a t-shirt, and if you finish, you get a finisher's jersey and plaque!

FIRST ATTEMPT

It was time to lay the groundwork for RAAM. To race RAAM solo, one must first qualify in order to show the race organizers that you may have a chance to finish. Since there was a qualifying race in Sebring, Florida, near where I lived, in Melbourne, I decided to enter that one. To qualify in Sebring, one needed to ride at least 400 miles in 24 hours. Sebring was the perfect choice for me. It was flat, fast, and had a favorable format for an analytic mind. It starts with an out and back leg of about 100 miles, followed by ten mile laps until 6:30 pm, at which time it moves onto the Sebring race track for 12 hours of 3.75 mile laps. It makes the math easy for computing one's progress, and breaks the race down into manageable sections. Although the weather is usually mild with calm winds, I have yet to experience that in my three races there. It was always cold and windy. My plan was to ride the first 100 as fast as I could to get ahead of the curve, ride the ten mile laps at a measured pace, then see what I needed to do for the remaining 12 hours in order to make the qualifying mileage. The race requires support, so I coerced Earl Bradley, a fellow racer on the same mountain bike team, not to mention a good mechanic, into going with me to serve in that capacity. My needs during the first half of the race were minimal, and once we moved onto the track, they became even less, this made it a boring affair for Earl, so we were reduced to finding comic relief with the wind induced problems a fared recumbent was having. It was a recumbent bike enclosed in a shell for aerodynamics. Earl was stationed in the pit area next to the recumbent's support crew who were in radio contact with their rider. I was behind their rider, whom we nicknamed "The Egg" because of his appearance, on the track, when I saw a gust of wind take him down. Like a turtle, he was helpless. Earl heard the radio transmission from the rider to his crew, so as I passed Earl in the pits, he delighted in proclaiming, "The Egg is down!". As the evening wore on, I continually did the calculations to see what average I needed to stay above in order to reach my goal of 400 miles. This technique would come into play later, when I was racing RAAM. Once I had that number down to 7mph, I started to breathe a little easier. That would give me a cushion in the event of a time consuming mechanical delay, or even a bio-mechanical issue. Neither of those took place, so I managed to finish with 430 miles. My overconfidence received an un-needed boost. That's when I decided it was time to enter RAAM. Preparations went well for my first attempt in 2011. My crew was in place, travel plans had been made, my fitness was good, and our expectations high. What could possibly go wrong? We were starting this race as minimalists. A crew of four, and only two SUV's. The plan was to estimate how far I was going to get in each stretch, and get a hotel. While good in theory, it was not a good plan. Turns out, when the body says "sleep", it doesn't care if you are at the hotel or not. As a result, we either had to stop before I needed, or shuttle to the hotel, sleep, then shuttle back to the exact spot on the route to restart. Time is critical in RAAM, and that was wasted time.

The race starts at an awkward time in Oceanside. Racers are staggered at intervals, since drafting is not allowed, and it commences in the afternoon. Since "race time" is EDT, it is even later in the afternoon on the race clock. It is hard to establish any kind of sleep schedule, so our plan was to go for at least 36 hours to try and force some kind of schedule. That would also get me through much of the desert at night when it was cooler. One hundred degrees is, after all, cooler than one fifteen. The first stint went well, and I actually felt pretty good when I went down for my first break. After what I thought was a four hour nap, I set out on leg two. This session felt pretty good as well, so we limited my next break to two hours. As I started round three, I couldn't figure out why I was feeling so sluggish. I had worked a schedule similar to this in the past, and had felt better. That was when, after discussing with Steve Lufkin, my crew chief, that we realized there had been a misunderstanding. When I had asked for the four hour, and subsequent two hour break, I had meant four and two hours of sleep. He had made the actual breaks that long. He told me that my actual sleep had been two hours the first break, and 45 minutes the next. The rest of the break time was wasted in shuttle and set up time.

Although I was now behind the power curve regarding sleep, we had Durango in our sights, so spirits were high. Durango was the first intermediate time cut-off station, and represented one third of the way through. I was actually looking forward to the next three mountain climbs after Durango, beginning with Wolf Creek Pass, the highest point in the race. It was during the ascent of the third pass, Cochura, when things started to unravel. It was the middle of the night, cold, and windy. The undulations on the way to the top were unrelenting. It was taking forever. I was tired, and starting to feel the accumulated effects of some poor planning. The first issue was nutrition. I have a hard time with solid food when I ride, so was relying on a liquid diet. I was getting the calories, and electrolytes, but little else. I was not taking in needed vitamins, minerals, and most importantly, general nutrition. As a result, my body was starting to metabolize muscle for fuel. The second, and most critical mistake, was underestimating the importance of massage. As a result, I was starting to accumulate lactic acid. That, and some high altitude edema, had caused my legs to swell to twice their normal size. I looked like a speed skater! This was a recipe for disaster. Disaster soon came. On some climb after Cochura Pass, I went to push a pedal stroke in a gear too big, and it felt as though my right quad had exploded. The pain was so great, that I could not even ride with my right leg clipped into my pedal. I was forced to pedal with my right leg hanging uselessly beside the bike. This would, of course been a perfect time to stop, but we were all sleep deprived, and never really considered it. We had an unusually strong tail wind, and thought maybe we could "ride through it". We tried several different wrapping techniques, and even called my physician for a prescription for Voltarin, a topical pain reliever, like Ibuprofin. We took an extended break, hoping I could recover, and miraculously, I did (somewhat). At this point, I had no idea how we were doing with regard to time limits. They would just put me on my bike, and I would ride.

We somehow made it through Kansas, but then somewhere in Missouri, reality started to set in. St. Louis was the second intermediate time cut off, and Steve realized that we probably were not going to make it. As I sat by the side of the road, taking a break, just short of St. Louis, he came and sat beside me. "Marshall, I don't think we're going to make the second cut off." I remember my shock as I was forced, for the first time, to consider that I was not going to finish. I'll never know if he was using reverse psychology or not, but once my initial shock wore off, I became angry. He said, "We can throw in the towel now, but if you want to try, we're with you." Back on my bike, with new focus, I set off for St. Louis. In reality, I would never have made it if not for some last minute good fortune.

During the race, the race directors are constantly updating the crews with regard to changes in the route due to road construction, and other impediments to the original route. As we approached St. Louis, we received one such notification which allowed us to put me in the car and drive the last five miles to the time station. Since we made the cut off by less than an hour, that last minute change was the only way we were able to do it. Having dodged that bullet, we were now two thirds of the way through, and celebrated with a big meal (my first since the start) from Applebee's. RAAM is a series of ups and downs, and after our previous "down", this was a much needed "up". After another much needed sleep break, we knew we still had another 1000 miles to go, so once again, we got on the road.

Although my leg was better, we had lost a great deal of time, and were still dealing with the accumulated effects of sleep deprivation. The stress of physical injury, which now included saddle sores, only made it worse. (One lesson learned: When applying chamois butter onto open sores due to chafing, don't mistake the mentholated version for the original). Throughout the entire race, we had taken great pleasure in ticking off each state as we entered and departed. A special "salute" with each milestone. We were now able to "salute" Missouri, Illinois, Indiana, and finally Ohio. As we entered Ohio, however, the math didn't lie. In order to successfully complete RAAM, one needs an overall speed average of 10.0 mph. That includes all of the "down" time. As we passed time station 42 in Blanchester, Ohio, our average had dropped to 9.9 mph. Had I been fresher, I may have been able to pick it up and improve that average, but that was not the case. As I left the McDonald's that served as that time station, encouraged by the incredible cheers from the people who man time station 42, even in the middle of the night, I looked down at my computer and, although I felt as though I was going at least 20 mph, saw that I was in fact, only going 12 mph. I tried to pick up the pace, but was unable. After a few more miles, I called to Steve, driving the follow car, and broke the news. We were done. 2426 miles ridden. 563 miles short of our goal of Annapolis. As we drove away in silence, the extent of our efforts became starkly apparent, as Steve fell asleep at the wheel, and nearly drove straight through a curve. The blaring horn of the oncoming car woke us both up.

REFLECTIONS

The reality of failure is a difficult pill to
swallow, and one not often endured by myself
or Steve. Once we finished licking our wounds,
we started to analyze our efforts to see where
we needed to improve if we ever were to try it
again, which of course, we were. Our biggest
mistake was to go without an RV. Trying to
stay in hotels was just too time consuming and
impractical. Additionally, we underestimated
the effects of sleep deprivation on the crew.
Lack of sleep for the rider is a given, but we
didn't realize how it affects the rest of the crew
as well. RAAM is one of those athletic events
which is truly a team effort. Each member

being equally important, not just the rider. A crew of four is just not enough. Other considerations were the need for a massage therapist, and better monitoring of proper nutrition. Finally, we realized we needed better funding.

As time passed, a plan started to come together. In an effort to allow me to concentrate on just riding, Steve took everything on himself. He put a crew of seven together, solicited funding, reserved an RV, arranged for vehicles to arrive at the start, and told me to just ride my bike and be ready. It was now looking like 2014 would be our next attempt. My fitness was good, but I decided to requalify at Sebring again, just to compare this year to 2011. Although conditions were much worse, with temperatures dropping to 30 degrees, and the wind howling at 25 mph, with gusts to 35, my results were similar to that of 2009. We were RAAM ready. Having analyzed our first effort to identify our mistakes, we were determined not to repeat those, but to discover new ones.

RAAM 2014 started well, or so I thought. In an effort to allow me to concentrate on riding my bike, and not worry about anything else, Steve instituted an isolation policy. No one was to tell me how I was doing by comparison to other racers, or if anything was going awry with the crew. I reluctantly went along, but in retrospect, realize that I need to be proactive in order to perform at my best. An incident with the RV on the first day nearly ended our bid before we had really started. On parts of the course, because of roads and conditions, the RV is not allowed. It must be driven to a point on the race course further along by an alternate route. Our RV wound up on a restricted section of the course. After a great deal of negotiating with race officials, Steve was able to talk us out of a

"DQ" (disqualification). The concession was that the individual who had been driving the RV, would not be allowed to drive any more. This meant that Steve was now the only one on the crew able to drive the RV from that point on. The effects of that would manifest later in the race. Weather is always a factor in RAAM, and this year was not very nice to us.

It was hotter than usual in the desert, but more importantly, it was windy in Kansas. Not the nice tailwind as in 2011, but a brutal cross/head wind. Kansas is flat, so there is nothing to slow the wind down. Kansas is also dusty, so the wind picks up the sand and pelts you with it. It was so bad, that it sand blasted the paint off of my spokes, and destroyed my bike's drive train. The worst thing it did, however, was to put me, and everyone else, behind schedule. Times are not adjusted due to adverse weather conditions, so we just had to press harder, as did everyone else. We were still going well, and actually made it toward St. Louis in much better shape than the first time. Unfortunately, this meant that we were dipping into the well a little too deeply. It would eventually catch up with us.

As we approached St. Louis, one of RAAM's little anomalies became agonizingly apparent. For some reason, the race director likes to put in some convoluted twists in the route. Nearing the Mississippi River, we started to take several seemingly unnecessary turns as we approached the time station. We could see that there was a much more direct route, yet we were taking the scenic version, only there was not much to see on the Mississippi flood plain. It was hot, I was exhausted, and it was here that my race almost ended. I previously mentioned the three types of sleep I experienced; total, sleepwalking, and dream. As I droned on down yet another needless route diversion, riding with my arms resting on my aerobars, I absolutely fell asleep. Somehow, I awoke as I was falling, in time to catch myself. The extra shot of adrenaline of that close call, actually helped get me to the time station. Ironically, when I got there, I saw another rider already there, whom I had passed much earlier. Apparently he found a shorter route.

Leaving St. Louis, I was in much better shape than I was the first time. Unfortunately, not so much Steve. As grueling as being crew chief is, add to that having to drive an RV across the country at a snail's pace by yourself, as he was still the only one authorized to drive due to our day one hiccup. In order to get some rest, he would drive to the next time station, and wait for me while trying to get some rest himself. This negated the effectiveness of having an RV, and forced me to try to get to each subsequent time station to rest, as opposed to stopping when I needed to. Same as

2011. We still managed to sail through Illinois and Indiana, with only one minor setback.

My 'biking while asleep' just short of St. Louis was not my only experience with an unexpected shot of adrenaline during this race. As I noted, fatigue was as much a factor for the crew as it was for the rider. Imagine pacing someone on a bike, riding for hours behind them going a pedestrian 15-20 mph. Even with two people in the car, it's nearly impossible to stay awake. We discovered just how hard that was. Somewhere in Indiana, at night, with nothing in the way of scenery other than one headlight illuminated cornfield after another, my race nearly ended for the second time. As I was grinding along, suddenly I heard my follow car's engine rev up as it accelerated behind me. I had just enough reaction time to aim toward the right side of the road before the car smashed into my rear wheel. I did a back flip over the front right fender, landing hard on my elbow in the gravel. They immediately stopped, expecting the worst. Miraculously I stood up with the only injury being a little road rash on my hip, and a small contusion on my elbow. My rear wheel was destroyed, but the only damage to my bike was a bent derailleur hanger. They were more shook up than I was. We didn't want to alarm the rest of the crew, so we fabricated a story about me hitting a rut in the road and crashing. I'm not sure everyone believed it, but no one questioned it. The only benefit was that shot of adrenaline, which enabled me to pick up my speed to the next time station. I was not sure how many of those "shots" I had left in me!

Although this part of the country is flatter than what we had thus far traversed, it was by no means flat. It served as a reminder of the Appalachian mountains, which were still to come. It was on one of these innocuous 'rollers' that I carelessly accelerated with no regard to pedaling form, and tweaked my right knee. I immediately flashed back to the injury during my first attempt, and nearly panicked. Please tell me it wasn't going to end again! As I carefully pressed on, it hurt, but was not debilitating. What a relief.

We had now passed Blanchester, Ohio, so were further along than we were the first time. There was something uplifting about seeing new sights. It was early afternoon when we once again got an unwanted dose of needless routing. For some reason, the race directors decided that we needed a scenic tour of the university campus in Athens, Ohio. Not only that, but it was mostly cobblestones. Not fun with another case of saddle sores. Once we got to that time station, I went for some medical treatment for my knee, which was still bothering me. I was exhausted, and fell asleep on the table. It was summertime in Ohio, so thunderstorms were starting to build as we prepared for our run to the next time station. Once there, we would be in West Virginia! Salute. This would have been the perfect time for me to get an extended break. I was extremely tired, it was storming, and the next segment was longer than most, taking us into the Appalachians.

As I lobbied for a break, Steve pointed out that we were behind schedule based on the expected arrival times to each time station as published in the back of the route book. Although this was printed in advance and didn't take into account weather conditions along the way (wind in Kansas), it was a convenient metric for two very tired people to use. Reluctantly, with rain pouring down, lightning flashing, and thunder booming, I acquiesced, and got back on my bike. Conditions were so bad, I opted for my back up cyclocross bike with fat knobby tires. This segment into West Union, West Virginia is 85 miles long. As night fell, it got foggy and drizzly. Barely able to keep my eyes open, I stopped frequently for combat naps. I would sit in the follow car, and try to get one REM cycle of about10-15 minutes, before getting back on my bike and pushing forward once again. As a result, the segment took me over ten hours. Now with no time to rest, we pushed on towards Grafton, W Va. My fatigue remained unabated, so I had to resort to more combat naps. It was here where the hills got ugly. Steep and frequent, I barely had the energy to get to the top of each one. As we plodded along Route 50 through the business district of a small town between West Union and Grafton, I got slower and slower. I'm sure Steve was agonizing over my progress as he waited in Grafton. As I was stopped for yet another short break in the parking lot of a small florist shop, Steve called. I was handed the phone, and Steve told me that the race officials had pulled me from the race. It was over, and I had been put out of my misery. As we drove to a rendezvous with Steve, I realized that my average was still above the threshold of 10.0 mph, so was unsure why the race officials had made that decision. When I called Steve to ask him about it, he said we would discuss it later. I started to think maybe Steve just told me that in order to get me to stop. He was done, and so was I, but without his decision, we would have suffered on until the clock ran out.

Adding insult to injury, we drove to the finish in Annapolis to recover, and to prepare the RV to turn in. It was there we had the bittersweet privilege of seeing all of those who had successfully completed the race. Another tough pill to swallow. From there we said our goodbyes, and Madge and I flew to North Carolina to recover. As I sat licking my wounds once again, I reflected on what went right, and what went wrong. We had gotten to within 250 miles of the finish. After two attempts, and nearly 5200 miles of RAAM, I had absolutely nothing to show for it. As we sat in a cabin in the mountains, overlooking Lake Fontana, Madge turned to me, and as disappointed as I was, said, "Well, I guess this means you'll have to try it again." We've been together a long time. She knows me too well.

THAT WHICH DOES NOT KILL ME...

I was now "0 for 2". Each time I had a plan, but as Mike Tyson, the heavyweight boxer, once said, "Everyone has a plan, until they get punched in the face." I had definitely been punched in the face twice now. As I looked throughout the history of RAAM, I was curious as to how many others had tried and failed. I was, of course, not alone. While many entered once, finished, and said "No more.", others tried several times before finishing. Still others tried multiple times, and never finished. I noted several agonizing cases of individuals getting to within as close as 50 miles, and falling short. I could certainly feel their pain. The race hadn't killed me yet, so I still had a chance. I felt as though the only way to fail was to quit trying.

Not a day went by when I did not think about the race. My biggest concern now was my age. I was now 58, and showing the signs of years of racing. I had no serious health issues, but several minor nagging ones. In RAAM, each of those could mean the difference between finishing and not. My goal was to try again in 2016 when I turned 60. RAAM was generous in that they gave us old folks an extra 21 hours in which to finish. I didn't want to have to use them, but it was nice to know they were there. In the meantime, I planned to train and race to see if I noted any serious drop off in my ability.

The experience from my first two attempts had taught me a great deal. I had the nutrition figured out. Since I can only tolerate liquids when I am riding the bike, I had started relying on meal replacement shakes, such as Ensure and Boost as my main source of food. Additionally, I had found good success in electrolyte replacement with "EmergenC". My goal was to use products that could be found in grocery stores along the way. That way, I would not have to worry about replacing proprietary products if I ran out during the race. I had also fallen in love with electronic shifting for my bikes. During RAAM 1, my left hand had gotten so weak during the race, that I could no longer shift into the big ring, the large front gear, without reaching around the brake hood, and pulling the lever toward the stem. Electronic shifting eliminated that problem. I was still trying to find a cure for saddle sores, but had two years to find the perfect saddle.

The hardest part for me in this, or any supported race, is finding support. I am not comfortable asking people to make such a huge sacrifice for me. If I can find a way to self support, I will. That works well even for 24 hour races involving multiple laps, such as Sebring, as long as I can figure out a way to set up a pit area with food and drinks. This issue, ironically, led to me acquiring a crew member who turned out to be invaluable in 2016. Assembling the crew for my first two attempts had been mostly left up to my crew chief, Steve Lufkin. He also handled most of the other details such as vehicles, and crew logistics. I never realized how daunting that responsibility was until I did it for myself in 2016. The catalyst for my third attempt came in the random offer from two friends to serve as crew. "Hey Marshall", texted Tyler Jandreau one day, "If you ever decide to do RAAM again, me and Joseph are in." Tyler and Joseph Joseph were two friends of mine, and good friends with each other. They were both avid cyclists and two of the smartest people I know. Perfect, I thought, that would be an ideal start to a crew. I now had the impetus to get the ball rolling.

Experience can never be discounted in an event such as this, so I reached out to my former crew chief, Steve Lufkin, to see if he was available. He gave me a tentative "yes" pending developments with his job. With my first two attempts, I came to the realization that RAAM is very similar to a military operation. Although I had served in the U.S. Navy as a pilot, the epitome of "military" would have to be the Navy SEAL. I happened to have two younger brothers who were Navy SEAL's. I reached out to Scott, living in San Diego, close to the start in Oceanside. He and his wife Lynda, had served as our "west coast base" for our first two attempts. He too, gave me an initial thumbs up, depending upon his job situation.

Next, I called my son, Jesse, to see if he was interested. He had crewed on our second attempt, and was as disappointed as I was in not finishing. He was a quick "in". I was now up to a certain three, and possibly five. I still needed a few more individuals willing to give three weeks of their lives for this dubious cause.

My highest priority was for a massage therapist, and possibly a nurse who could administer IV's to aid in recovery. My previous therapist was unavailable, so I was on the look out. I am part owner of 'Infinity Bike Shop', in Melbourne,

Florida, and as such, spend a lot of time there. Too much, says my wife, Madge. As fate would have it, I was there one day when Jim Merchant, new to Melbourne, walked in to browse. We started talking and I found out that he was an accomplished triathlete some twenty years ago, before a career change took him away from it. That career change happened to be to become both a massage therapist, and a registered nurse. Too good to be true. We hit it off, and the subject of RAAM came up. I told him I needed a massage therapist/nurse to crew for me, and for him to think about it and let me know, but he said, "I don't need to. I'm in."

Ideally, a RAAM crew consists of at least six people, sometimes more. I've seen as many as fifteen. To do it properly, one needs three vehicles. One RV, and two cars. Each vehicle requires two people, hence the magic number of six. Still, more is better, just more expensive, and RAAM is expensive enough as it is. I now had four confirmed, and two probables. It was now February and based on our progress, I felt comfortable in putting my entry in for the race in 2016. Details remaining included finding a mechanic, qualifying for the race, and procuring an RV. The RV is the greatest expense, since a one way rental with all the added mileage charges add up to about $10,000. I decided to try and buy one. I figured I could use it, and sell it at a loss after the race, and still be better off than renting. I decided on a Mercedes Sprinter platform, and even found a place to build it out as a camper. Unfortunately, the lead time was six months, so even though I thought I was ahead of the game, I was, in fact, not! I had to find one already built. Added to RV concern was the fact that I was hearing rumblings on the RAAM/ultracycling forum that RV's were becoming hard to find.

Living in Florida has many advantages. I can train year round, and there are a million places that sell RV's. I found exactly what I was looking for nearby in Fort Pierce. I wanted a new one to try and minimize issues involving a used one. It was a 22 foot Road Trek, E-Trek. All electric with no propane or generator to worry about. It was not cheap, but again, I had the option of selling it once the race was over. After two weekend trips with Madge, to learn the ropes, the RV situation was under control. All I really needed to do now was finalize the crew, and get qualified. Not so fast.

It was about at this time that Steve called to inform me that, due to his job, he would be unavailable to be on the crew. A big blow, but not totally unexpected. Unfortunately, I was about to get another blow. Early one Sunday in March, my phone rang, and I saw from the caller ID, that it was my brother, Scott. I knew what he had to say even before I answered. Sure enough, his employment had changed, and he lost all of his vacation. He would not be available to be on the crew either. I was now without a crew chief. I put the word out to the remaining crew members, and immediately Tyler nominated Joseph for the position. I quickly seconded the nomination, so the resolution passed without Joseph being afforded the opportunity to protest. He proved to be a solid choice (with Tyler as co-chief).

I had failed twice, and still felt as though I should be able to do it. In the words of a certain accomplished ultracyclist, Dex Tooke, it was "unfinished business", the title of his book. However, ego alone was not a good enough reason for me to attempt it again. I would certainly feel better about it if I could tie it to a worthwhile cause. One of the noteworthy aspects of RAAM, is that nearly every racer is riding to raise money for a charity, so it would certainly not be unprecedented for me to do the same Prior to the second attempt, I met Maria Parker. She and her husband Jim, had founded a charity to raise money to heighten awareness, and find a cure for brain cancer. Maria's sister had been diagnosed with the horrible disease prior to Maria's RAAM attempt in 2013 (which Maria won). Maria's sister lost her battle with the disease, but the charity she inspired lives on. I contacted Maria, and asked if she needed riders for the cause. She readily accepted my offer, and I now had a reason for RAAM. Maria, Jim, and their daughter, Lucia, were going to be in Sebring this year, which is where I had decided to try to qualify again for RAAM. We would work out the details there.

My decision to race for "3000 Miles To A Cure", Maria's charity, soon provided me an unexpected bonus. As we assembled for the race in Sebring, I had decided to ride it unsupported. The only problem with that was after 6 pm, when the race moves onto the actual race track. At this point, I would need someone to move my gear, from the outside of the track, into the pit area. That way I could grab food or drink, add clothing, and have access to spare bike parts if needed. I imposed upon Maria and her entourage for help. Jacob Bouchard was a member of that entourage, and he, along with Maria, Jim, and Lucia, agreed to help. Not only did they move my gear, they stayed through the night to lend support. It made for a much less stressful race. As a result, I was able to finish the race with enough miles to qualify for RAAM, and set a new age group record in the process. The real benefit of that experience, however, was that Jacob became interested in crewing for a RAAM racer, and asked if he could crew for me. His addition to the crew turned out to be one the most crucial.

There was one remaining hole in my crew composition; mechanic. I knew that minor repairs could be handled by several people already on the crew, specifically Joseph and Tyler, but a dedicated mechanic is a huge benefit. I had just about exhausted all my resources in my search for this final essential crew member when I saw a fortuitous posting on the RAAM/ultracycling forum. The forum is run by an individual by the name of Lee Kreider. He posts interviews, news, and opinion relating to the ultracycling community, with an emphasis on RAAM. On this occasion, he posted that Adam Darby, a bicycle mechanic in Athens, Ohio, might be available to crew for this year's RAAM. I responded immediately with a message to Adam, but got no response. I thought maybe I had been too late, when two weeks prior to the start of RAAM, he finally responded. He had been busy graduating from college, and had not had the time to reply sooner. He asked if I still needed a mechanic. I did, and now he was it, sight unseen. I told him to send me preferences, and I would arrange travel to Oceanside. Half joking, I added, "But if you want the full experience, I could fly you to Orlando, and you could help me drive the RV to the west coast." He responded with, "That sounds like fun." I quickly accepted that offer, and booked him to Orlando before he could change his mind. Another stroke of luck that turned out very well.

My luck continued as race day approached, when Maria called to see if I needed and more crew. An individual had expressed interest in crewing for Rob DeCou, the other "3000 Miles To A Cure" racer, but since Rob already had a full complement, they thought of me. I already had six crew members by this point, which was enough, but thought that one more would not hurt, so I accepted. I contacted Ryan Jean, my newest crew member, and we hit it off immediately. Over the phone, I found out that he was a true adventurer in search of another. He was fresh from an around the country bike tour, and had free time coinciding with RAAM. His only problem was that he would not be able to get to Oceanside until the day before the race. The day before the race is the most hectic, with all the meetings, pictures, gear inspections and credential verification, but we could somehow make it work. Although my brother, Scott, was unavailable to be on the crew, he became our San Diego to Oceanside shuttle service.

The start of RAAM was just around the corner, and everything was finally in place. The only real variable was the crew dynamics. There were now eight people involved in this project, and not a single individual knew all of the others. The crew now consisted of the following: Joseph Joseph, Tyler Jandreau, Jesse Reeves, Jim Merchant, Jacob Bouchard, Adam Darby, Ryan Jean, and myself. I knew Joseph, Tyler, Jesse, Jim, and Jacob. Joseph,

Tyler and Jesse knew each other, and that was it. No one else knew any of the others. With Ryan arriving the day before the start, I was sure that 24 hours would give us plenty of time to bond, and become the cohesive unit we would have to be in order to succeed in the "world's toughest bicycle race". Not really, but somehow, we would make it work!

PART TWO

RAAM 2016

The race was to start on Tuesday, June 14. Our time line was as follows. Jim Merchant was going to drive one car with most of the gear, including bikes, out the week before. I was going to drive the RV with a third car in tow, leaving on

Wednesday, June 8. My friend, Ross Parker, and I would stop in Orlando, pick up Adam Darby, and make our way west. Ross would leave us along the way in order to get back to work, and Adam and I would continue. Everyone else was flying in.

Joseph and Tyler would arrive a couple of days early, Jesse, two days prior, and Ryan arriving the day before the race.

I had to fly one more trip for my job as a pilot, to Frankfort, Germany and would get home Monday the 6th. Life as an international pilot actually helped prepare me for RAAM with regards to sleep deprivation and odd sleep cycles. Being six time zones away from home means sleeping when you have to, even if it means getting up at midnight, or sleeping at what is 4pm in your home time zone. That means you are sleeping when everyone you know is awake. Normally when I sleep, I turn my phone off so as not to be disturbed, but for some reason, this night I did not. Our run of good fortune ended abruptly when I was awakened with the buzz of an incoming text informing me that Jim Merchant did not make it to Oceanside: "Sir, this is Arcadio. Your friend have an accident on I-10. He's conscious, and on his way to the hospital."

I was now fully awake. The text had obviously been sent by someone at the accident scene using Jim's phone. I tried calling back, but got no answer. It was still early on the east coast, so I started making phone calls to try to get some answers. I relayed the sketchy information to Joseph, Ross, and Madge, hoping they could find out more. I didn't know where he was, what had happened, or how he was. There was nothing more I could do at this time, and I still had to fly an airplane full of people to Atlanta the next day, so I forced myself back to sleep, hoping to learn more the next day.

As I slept, the team at home was busy gathering information. Quickly touching base the next morning, prior to my flight, I learned that the accident had occurred near El Paso, Texas. The car with both bikes had been destroyed, and Jim was in the hospital in critical condition, with multiple injuries. I later learned from Jim, that a semi truck had crossed the center line, touched Jim's car, and flipped him. Jim, who remained conscious throughout, said he rolled four times, slid on the roof into the dirt, then rolled three more times before coming to rest upright. He suffered a broken eye socket, broken hip, broken clavicle, broken sternum, broken ribs, collapsed lung, and a lacerated liver. We also now knew that Jim was still in the ICU at the El Paso hospital. Nothing more could be done at this time.

I now had plenty to think about on the long flight home. For some reason, not racing never entered my mind. Nor did our sudden change in fortune dissuade any of the remaining six crew members. Jim, too, would hear none of that. Thank goodness we added Ryan Jean! All we had to do now was come up with another car, two bikes, and all the gear required for a 3000 mile bicycle race. We had taken months to get everything together the first time. I'm sure we could do it all again in less than a week. Although Jim's condition was rapidly improving, barring a miracle, we would additionally be without the services of our nurse/massage therapist, but we would just have to make do. We were mostly just happy that he was alive. Fortunately, as part owner of Infinity Bike Shop, in Melbourne, Florida, we had resources. Everyone at the shop was aware of what had happened, and took it upon themselves to make the bike problem disappear. When I showed up at the shop on Tuesday, the day before I was to leave, our mechanics, Lukas, Goeff, and Frank, had put together two replacement bikes. Lukas even brought from home, his collection of cold weather gear, since we didn't know what we would be able to salvage from the wreckage. I still had my original spare Eddy Merckx, Mouranx at home, but had never ridden it. I took it to the shop and quickly rode it, and the one that had been built up, for a few laps around the parking lot while Frank did some quick fit adjustments. Not perfect, but I would have 3000 miles to get used to it. I went on a quick shopping spree in the shop to collect replacements for everything else that had been in the car, loaded it all up, and hoped for the best. Months of planning, redone in two days.

Early the next morning, I said goodbye to Madge, and pulled away from my house in the RV, with the Suburu in tow. I picked up

Ross, and we headed to Orlando to look for a bicycle mechanic. I had never seen him, but bicycle mechanics have a certain "look", so I was sure it would be no problem to pick him out of the crowd in the arrivals section of the Orlando airport. It helped that he knew to look for an RV, with a car behind it. We spotted each other immediately. He hopped on board, and off we went. I was hoping for an uneventful trip, but it was not to be. Our bad luck was still with us.

Just prior to our departure, I scheduled an appointment for the RV at the dealer in Fort Pierce for a check, prior to our departure. Ross drove it down, and while en route, the "check engine" light came on. They ran the diagnostics, and determined that it was a clogged injector. They took care of it, but as I was driving it home, after picking it up the day before we were to leave, the light came back on. It would have been easy to assume that it was for the same thing, but I didn't want to take any chances, so I called the local Mercedes dealer to see if I could at least get the light checked to see what was causing it. They told me the best they could do was have me drop it off, and they might get to it the next day. That wouldn't work, as we were leaving that morning, so I decided to take a chance and hope the engine didn't disintegrate. As a precaution, after we picked up Adam, we stopped at an auto parts store to get an engine diagnostic computer, so we could possibly make our own determination as to the cause of the light. The results were inconclusive, but the light was not flashing, which would have indicated a more serious problem, so we pressed on.

Something new I had to learn about diesel engines, was that they require special exhaust fluid in order to reduce emissions. As we proceeded west, the exhaust warning illuminated in addition to the "check engine" light. I checked the exhaust fluid level, and it was full, so we had no idea as to the cause. We would have pressed on, but in order to keep someone from driving with a faulty exhaust system, the engine is limited to ten starts before it resorts to a "fail safe" mode, which limits the forward speed to a mere 5mph. Just enough to exit the highway.

We were now just east of Baton Rouge, and down to 6 starts. Time for a pit stop. We called the Baton Rouge Mercedes dealer, and they were kind enough to squeeze us in that day. Four hours later, we were back on the road with a new "knock" sensor. The cause of both the "check engine' light, and the exhaust system fault. The only benefit to the lost time, was peace of mind with the RV and the discovery of a really good barbecue restaurant!

As we proceeded west, the crew was in constant contact trying to adjust for the loss of both a crew member, and a car. We were able to find the wreckage and its contents about 100 miles east of El Paso. Miraculously, we were able to salvage a good portion of the contents of the vehicle, although both bikes were completely destroyed. We were in contact with Jim by now, and he was doing better by the day. He was hopeful that, as a nurse, he would know all the right things to say in order to secure his release by the time we got to El Paso. We made it to San Antonio on Thursday, where we spent the night, and had to say goodbye to Ross at the airport, who had run out of time, and needed to get home. The next day, Adam and I pressed on to El Paso, where we found a hotel, and plotted with Jim to secure his escape. The earliest he could get released was Saturday morning, so Adam and I had another day of bonding over beer and barbecue in El Paso. Early Saturday morning, I drove to the hospital, where Jim was finishing up the remainder of his discharge paperwork. Once out, it was into the car, and straight to the pharmacy for a plethora of antibiotics and pain killers. It had been less than a week since Jim's accident, and he probably should still have been in the hospital. Not only was he out, he was trying to determine if it was at all feasible to function as a crew member for the race.

As we pressed westward to California, with Adam at the wheel, and Jim moaning with pain in the back of the RV, I was busy working the phone with Joseph, trying to determine if it was possible to complete RAAM with only one car. One of the determining factors, besides already having a minimum crew, was that the Suburu had a manual transmission. That would make it difficult to follow me on the bike at such slow speeds. Having already been run over once by the follow car, I decided we needed a replacement car. Rather than renting one, I decided since I was going to have to replace my wrecked car anyway, I would buy a new car now. I was looking for a small SUV, and after some research of what was available near Oceanside, decided on a BMW X1. I had Joseph research local BMW dealerships near Oceanside looking for one. Once he forwarded the findings of his search to me, I made phone calls to each of two dealerships. The first salesman was not impressed with the urgency of our situation, and said he would get back to me. At the second dealership, closer to Oceanside, I spoke to a salesman, Francisco, who happened to be familiar with RAAM, and was more than willing to help. As we spoke on the phone, he walked into the lot and found the perfect car. Thank goodness for the digital age, as we were able to complete the entire transaction, including financing, over the phone. I just hoped my insurance company was going to cooperate! I arranged to pick the car up on

Sunday, the next day. Francisco even vowed to show up for the start of the race the following Tuesday!

OCEANSIDE, CALIFORNIA

Adam, Jim, and I pulled into Oceanside late Saturday night, three days before the start of the race. We had new bikes, a new car ready for pick up, most of the gear we had salvaged from the wreckage, and most of the six crew members. We had survived a car wreck and a cross country journey with a faulty RV. Other than that, everything was going smoothly. A quick search of an on-line booking site secured a room at the Quality Inn, and we checked in. Tomorrow would be a new day, but now we needed sleep. I let Adam and Jim share the room, and I slept in the RV out in the parking lot. I figured Adam, as young as he was, could sleep through Jim's fitful night. I discovered how true that was, when the next morning, Jim was nowhere to be found. Apparently, he was in so much pain, he went to the hospital early that morning, with Adam none the wiser. With no way to check on Jim, I just had to hope he would contact me when he could. We had enough to do anyway. I had to get the car, and find my crew. Adam was with me, Joseph, Tyler, and Jacob were in nearby hotels, Jesse was due in that day, and Ryan was scheduled in Tuesday morning. We also had to do all the necessary race prep, such as marking the vehicles, and bikes, attend mandatory meetings, get everything inspected, attend a photo session, and pick up last minute items we would need for the race. In a way, that was good, in that we did not have time to think of how woefully unprepared we were turning out to be. First on the agenda that Sunday morning, was a meeting with the "3000 Miles to a Cure" team. In addition to Maria and Lucia, they had with them two complete media teams. One for each rider, myself and Rob DeCou. Each of us would be followed by a team to chronicle our progress, and keep supporters updated along the way. The tone of our adventure was on full display that morning. While Rob's crew was all business, ours was the complete opposite. As we tried to shake the cobwebs from our journey up to this point, my crew members were trying to get to know each other, as most of them had never met. It was then that I realized that it was going to work out fine. Each member of my crew seemed to instantly connect. Close in age, they had many of the same interests, and shared too many of the same movie quotes. Joseph, the crew chief, was trying to establish his role as leader by laying out some ground rules as to who would be doing what during the race. At an imposing 6'5", that was pretty easy. Well, it would have been, had it not been for Tyler. Tyler, an engineer, was only serious when he had to be. Apparently, this was not one of those times. As Joseph addressed each person, Tyler provided the comic relief. They have been friends for a long time, so Joseph took it in stride. Tyler's partner in crime was my son, Jesse. They had known each other for a long time as well, and although Jesse was now living on the opposite coast, in Portland, they fed off of each other like a well practiced comedy duo. Although new to the group, Adam, recent college graduate, and now our head mechanic, jumped in with both feet, verbally sparring with both Tyler, and Jesse, and holding his own quite well. Meanwhile, Jacob, another engineer, was probably wondering what he had gotten himself into. This was going to be a lot different from our initial introduction in Sebring. Always thinking, Jacob was going to turn out to be our "fixer". He had a solution for everything. This was two days before the race, so I just stayed in the background, soaking it all in, trying to think of anything we might have forgotten.

One of the first items for business in that meeting that morning, was for Maria and Lucia to explain our cause, and how it had originated. I watched my crew's riveted faces as Maria told the story of how brain cancer had taken the life of her sister, Jenny. You could not help but to be touched. The final brushstroke was when Jenny's son, Joe, told how he had been affected. Still a young man at 16, he had matured beyond his years by having lost his mother at such a young age. His comments, and blog posts during the race were inspirational. This cause, "3000 Miles to a Cure", proved to be our greatest motivation.

As ambassadors for this great cause, Maria explained what was expected of us. This included spreading the word through the wearing of "3000 Miles to a Cure" t-shirts, and distributing stickers. Our goal was to raise $20,000 for each rider, myself and Rob. Once these preliminaries had been taken care of, it was time to go around the room and have everyone introduce themselves, make a few comments, and to break the ice, name a guilty food pleasure to hopefully enjoy during the race. We started at the opposite side of the room with Rob's massive (by comparison) crew, and that was a bad thing. It gave my crew time to think of the most irreverent things they could possibly say. My cringe factor rose exponentially as we got closer to us. I can't recall a single specific comment that was made, but remember looking at Rob and his crew, and getting the impression that they were not overly confident of our chances. It did not appear as though we were taking this thing too seriously. On a brighter note, it gave us the opportunity to meet the members of our media crew. Our photojournalist was Bryan Cereijo. Although still in school, he proved himself to be capable beyond his years of experience. He is responsible for some incredible pictures of our journey. We also met Aly Moser, our blogger, and Luke Rafferty, our videographer. If it were not for them, I would have very little tangible recollection of RAAM. I was able to look on Facebook after the fact, relive the experience, and fill in some gaps. We also met members of Rob's crew, which included brothers, Chris and Tyler Clemens. They were responsible for procuring for us our final crew member, Ryan Jean, due to arrive the morning of the race. In an ironic twist, Chris and Tyler would play an integral part in our success, later in the race. Once the meeting was over, as most of the crew was making preparations for the upcoming inspections, I got a ride to the BMW dealership to pick up the car. As I drove out of the lot, I realized that this would be my only chance to enjoy that new car smell. Once it got to Annapolis, that smell would be long gone. That afternoon, a friend of Rob's was kind enough to invite everyone to a barbeque at their home. It was another chance for the teams to get to know each other, and more importantly, to keep our minds off of our upcoming race. Rob had never attempted the race before, but I had twice, and memories of the pain were starting to come back to me. It also provided an opportunity for me to spend a little time with my brother, Scott, who was picking Jesse up from the airport, and meeting us at the dinner.

Back in Oceanside that evening, I realized we still needed hotel rooms! The closest, and nicest hotel, and the one in which we were having our meetings, was the Spring Hill Suites. In another stroke of good fortune, after all that had gone wrong, I decided to try there first. I figured since Oceanside was near San Diego, a big military town, and close to Camp Pendleton, a Marine base, maybe they would have a military rate. Since I am technically still in the Navy reserves, I thought I would try. I walked to the desk, and asked, "Would you happen to have any availability for the next two nights, and do you have a military rate?" She answered yes to both, and when I heard the great room rate, I decided to spring for two rooms in order to give us a little more space. Not only was it a nice hotel, but it was within walking distance of all of the race venues. If only parking were so easy! Parking tickets turned out to be an additional burden on the budget, as we had three vehicles, and the parking lots were confusing at best. I hope the city of Oceanside put the money to good use.

The next day, after our team meeting, we got busy preparing for inspections. I mostly tried to stay out of the way, and keep my mind off of the race. Inspections are tedious, but important. Mostly for safety, but also for race and charity branding. This meant the application of numerous decals on all three vehicles, and the attaching of safety lights and reflectors. One of the items required was a set of flashing yellow lights to be magnetically placed on the back of each vehicle. When we salvaged our gear from the wrecked car, we could only find one of those flashing lights. When we went to registration, we were told that there were no additional ones available. We did a quick search of local auto parts stores, but came up empty. We had to get creative in order to buy time, as each team was scheduled to be inspected at a preset time. The media team's cars had to be inspected as well, and they were scheduled first. Once they passed their inspections, we removed their flashing lights, and transferred them to our vehicles just prior to the inspectors getting to them. We would still need the lights prior to the race start, but at least we got through the stressful inspections. The race director, Rick Boethling, eventually loaned us a set for the race, making us promise to return them to him in Annapolis. (Rick, I still have your lights, I'll get them to you next June.)

After inspections, Joseph, Tyler and I decided to go for an easy ride over the first part of the race course, just to calm our nerves, and make sure we knew the route for the first part, as this would be unescorted for me. We got lost. No, really, we got lost. We took a wrong turn, and would up at Camp Pendleton. We backtracked and found our mistake, but it didn't really do much to calm my nerves. I remember being nervous about the route in my other two attempts, but that they had course marshals out to make it easier, so I was hoping for the same this time.

That evening, we planned to meet for our last relaxed meal before all hell broke loose. Since this would be our last chance to drink before Annapolis (race rules), we opted for a Mexican restaurant with a two for one margarita special. I had been in contact with Jim, and told him we would be there if he could manage to join us. Injured or not, he was still a part of the crew. Our table was upstairs, and I couldn't mask my surprise when Jim came limping up the stairs to join us. This, barely a week removed from a horrendous car accident, resulting in multiple injuries, and only two days out of the hospital. I was glad to see him, but it was then that I realized that maybe things happen for a reason. One of the things that made this crew work so well together was the fact that they were all close in age. Jim was 59, Steve in his 50's, and my brother was 58. Although I was 60, I would just be the guy on the bike. Having a crew all close in age was probably better. I'm sure it would have been fine, but at this point, I was just trying to rationalize our bad luck, and keep the good vibe going.

THE RACE

I woke up on race morning having slept surprisingly well. I knew I would only get about three or four hours of sleep a night, at best, for the next twelve days, so my restful night was a welcome relief. Now awake just hours before my scheduled start, I began to get an uncharacteristic case of nerves. In the quiet time prior to the start, with all of the crew, including Ryan, who had flown in that morning, all busy with last minute preparations, I was alone in my hotel room with just my thoughts. I was reliving the pain and failure of my past RAAM attempts, trying to convince myself that this time I would succeed. Regardless, there was no turning back now. My most effective mental exercise in order overcome these doubts was to envision the finish and know that each step along the way was leading to that moment. Mentally, I was ready. Physically, we would see.

When I finally made my way downstairs, I met Ryan Jean for the first time. He had already integrated himself nicely with the rest of the crew, and was everything I had envisioned from our phone conversations. We were now a tight crew of six, plus one rider, ready to get this race underway. Each racer is given a specific start time based on their race number. You are given a race number the first time you ever enter RAAM, and you keep that number for life. When I raced in 2011, I was given number "417". I would start with that same number today. Start times are predicated on these race numbers in reverse order, so having a relatively low number meant that I would be going out late. Race time is always Eastern Daylight time, so my 2pm PDT start time was really 5pm 'race time'. This doesn't seem significant, except that our strategy was to get on a sleep schedule with a down time from around 1am, to 5am. I knew there was no way I would be ready to sleep that night after only 8 hours of riding, so we would have to improvise. In previous attempts, I rode far too long on my initial ride, got behind the sleep power curve, and eventually paid the price. This year we would ride smarter. I would ride long enough to enable me to sleep, and try to bend the times after a few days to the desired schedule. At least that was the plan.

I eventually made my way to the start area about an hour before my start. My brother was there, and I was glad to see him. He had been through SEAL "Hell Week", so he knew what I was about to endure. As promised, Francisco was there as well, from the BMW dealership. He even brought me a BMW t-shirt for good luck, so I gave him a "3000 Miles to a Cure" t-shirt in exchange. The tension at the start was palpable. You could see it on the faces of all the solo RAAM and RAW (race across the west) racers. Crews were giddy, and spectators, many of whom had no idea what was going on, were gathered to watch the spectacle. As each racer's time came near, his follow car assembled in the cue. Meanwhile, Jacob and I tried to get our communication system working. I don't know what made me think that it would. Oh well, another bridge to cross. We were going racing!

When my name was called, I rolled up on the start ramp. I was suddenly calm, as I knew we had made all the preparations we could, and that now it was all up to execution.....and luck. I remember idle conversation with the starter as we awaited the countdown. My final words to him as the countdown began was, "See you in

Annapolis." "Three, two, one.....", we were underway.

SESSION ONE

Although this was technically "day one", the nature of the race does not lend itself to thinking of it in terms of days. It is really one long day broken up by a few naps. By the end, no one really knows what day it is anyway, least of all me.

So for the sake of clarity in my mind, this was the beginning of "session one". Session one begins as a neutral roll out on a bike path for 8 miles. Passing is not allowed, so if you do, you will just be detained at the end of this section until the time when you were supposed to have gotten there. As a result, I knew that when I was passed by a racer who started behind me, he would be stopped, and order would be restored. These are, after all, rules, and not suggestions. At the end of this parade route, the race officially begins. It will be another 15 miles before you will see your support crew, so you must be prepared to handle any mechanical problem should it occur. This is a nervous time, as you are also responsible for staying on course. After getting lost on the pre-ride, this was certainly on my mind.

Fortunately, at this point in the race, you are usually within sight of other racers, so if you are lost, so are they. It is still a relief when you finally reach the left turn on Old Castle Road, and catch sight of your support vehicle.

There is no "easing into" this race. After the 8 miles of flat bike path, the hills begin in earnest. Within the first 57 miles to the first time station at Lake Henshaw, there are several climbs and descents of up to 8%. In fact, by mile 77, the route goes from sea level to an elevation of 4,227 feet! That point marks the first milestone of the race. It is the beginning of the descent of the "glass elevator". In just twenty miles, you will give up more than 3000 feet of elevation that you so painstakingly fought to gain. The view is spectacular. The desert floor is visible from the top, and you can see the heat shimmering from the scorching sand below. It may be only 5 miles away as the crow flies, but the cyclist, constrained by gravity and asphalt, makes up the 15 mile difference with tightly twisting switchbacks while buffeted by ever changing wind gusts. You can't win

RAAM in the first 100 miles, but you can certainly lose it. I enjoy descending, so I view it as a challenge. If I see someone in front of me, I make it a point to try to catch them. "Ducks on the pond". I recall glancing at my speedometer several times, and seeing 55 mph. I am still cautious, however, as there have been several spectacular crashes on this descent through the years. In my first attempt in 2011, I rounded a bend about half way down in time to see one such crash victim being loaded into an ambulance.

At the bottom of the descent is the desert town of Borrego Springs. It is a good spot to resupply, evaluate your physical and mental state, discuss plans with the crew, and brace yourself for the long desert crossing. Reality is now setting in. Memories of races past become vivid with the familiar sights and smells of the desert, and I can't help but to be reminded of the pain that is to come. The only way through it is to think about finishing. Start from the end, and work your way back. Break it down into manageable segments. At 100 miles, we are already 1/30th of the way done!

The desert heat and lack of humidity can easily derail even the fittest of competitors. It is here when respiratory ailments begin, only to cruelly manifest somewhere in the high elevations of the Rockies. Constantly breathing the hot dry air irritates the lungs. The wind and sun scorch the skin. There is no benefit to sweating. The air is so dry that sweat sublimates, and offers no cooling. Core temperatures can reach dangerous levels. Dehydration and electrolyte deficiencies can cause the body to shut down without warning.

All in all, the desert is a very unforgiving environment. There are obviously several things that can be done to mitigate the conditions, but none are foolproof. Ice packs, cooling vests, and water sprays are helpful. Scheduling the intake of fluids is a primary directive of the crew. One measure I had never considered was suggested to me by Ryan. That was the use of a "buff". I actually didn't know what it was prior to now. It is a thin cloth tube that fits over the head and around the neck. It can be pulled up over the nose and mouth to keep the dust out, and actually provide some moisture from exhalation. He happened to have one with him, which he let me use. It may have saved my lungs.

Fifty miles past Borrego Springs is the second time station (T2), in Brawley, Ca. It is between these two cities, Borrego Springs and Brawley, that the race passes it lowest point near the Salton Sea, which is actually below sea level. This is also the point where the crews start to get into a rhythm. By now, the adrenaline has mostly worn off, and natural pairings start to form. Joseph, being an observer by nature, was now able to ascertain individual strengths and personalities. Since there are always two crew members in the follow car, it is essential that they are capable, between them, to handle anything that may come up. It is also essential that they are able to tolerate each other in close quarters, for hours at a time, under stressful circumstances. There are also natural pairings based on who can stay awake the best in the middle of the night. Pairings can, and should change, but for now we seemed to have an efficiently functioning team. Joseph and Tyler were a natural fit, as were Ryan and Adam, the "Hair Team". Both sporting long flowing locks, of which, being follically challenged, I was just a little jealous. Jesse and Jacob also fit together well. Not only because they shared the letter "J", but also because their passion and strengths complemented each other nicely. Jacob was the "McGyver", coming up with solutions to whatever went wrong, and Jesse was good at keeping my spirits up in the dark times. I am usually pretty easygoing, but I did have my moments, such as my "diva" episode, late in the race, when I pitched a fit when I did not get the Chili Mac I had been craving for my break meal. Or so I am told.

We were now solidly into the race, and the calculations began. Joseph and Tyler started plotting progress, keeping our running average speed, anticipated breaks, and sections that could result in slower than expected speeds. The clock does not stop, so when we take a break, our average goes down. We also started tracking nutrition and hydration. I was "old school", and as such did not run a heart rate monitor, or power meter. Those tools would have make it much easier to track how the rider is responding. I was without, and it just made it harder for the crew to gauge my condition. Even so, they did a great job in keeping the machine humming along. The only downside to a smoothly running operation, is that it never stays that way. This race would be no exception.

The conditions of the desert take a toll not only on the rider, but the equipment as well. Dirt and dust contaminate the bike's drive train, and the heat makes the vehicles work harder. We were already having issues with the RV. The state of the art electrical system was starting to malfunction. The RV was being powered by lithium batteries which were being recharged by the engine, and solar panels. It was all controlled through an inverter to run all of the creature comforts. All good in theory until the inverter starts popping circuit breakers, rendering it inoperable. Even calls to the manufacturer failed to provide the guidance necessary to keep the system running properly. This issue would plague us throughout the race. Just one more obstacle to overcome.

With the Glass Elevator in the rear view mirror, we were now focused on our next milestone, the end of the desert. This was just a section to get through. Although beautiful in its own way, it is marked by long straight flat roads, and hellish temperatures. Every time you stop, you think you are in a blast furnace. Inspiration here comes from anticipating something so simple as a chance to make a turn. It's the little things at this point. One reward for completing this section, is the festive atmosphere of the time station at the end. They always have a wading pool filled with cold water, and of course, popsicles. It's a treat for both rider and crew. Time stations are a big part of RAAM. Many, such as this one, are manned. Usually by the same people year after year. They go out of their way to provide comfort to the participants. Many are themed, such as the pirate station near the end of the race. Many open their homes up to the crew to provide a few luxuries, such as showers, which are infrequent at best. These stations are manned 24 hours a day, since riders come through at all times. RAAM would not be RAAM without the dedicated people manning these time stations.

As we said goodbye to California, and hello to Arizona, we braced ourselves for one of the most difficult sections of RAAM. From below sea level, we make our way to an elevation of over six thousand feet. This would be our environment, with a few respites of around 3000 feet, over the next few days, all the way through Kansas. We gain this elevation, sometimes gradually and imperceptibly, but usually abruptly and painfully. To make matters worse, with the thin dry air, you can see the climbs from miles away, giving you plenty of time to think about them. Yarnell grade is one such climb, rising 1800 feet in just 7 miles. As if this is not enough, it was here we received our first curve ball from the race directors. They decided just before the race start to alter the route in this section to one with less traffic. This resulted in the addition of nearly 100 miles. Most of it one hill after another. No compensation was made in regards to time, so everyone's calculations were forced to be adjusted. This amounted to anywhere from six to eight hours of additional riding to make the first time cut off in Durango. As hard as this was on us, it was harder on the RAW (Race Across the West) riders, as they followed the same route, and were finished in Durango. Everyone, however, was racing under the same rules, so we just accepted it.

With this additional time constraint being imposed upon us we knew the breaks had to be shorter, and the riding faster. I had taken an early break this year, trying to stay ahead of the fatigue, so we were even more anxious. One realization I had was that I needed an easier gear for the bike. With fatigue setting in, and even harder climbs coming up in Colorado, the gearing I had was going to be difficult. The only benefit of the altered route was that the RV had a shorter way to get to Flagstaff. This enabled Adam to get there, find a bike shop, and procure a new rear cassette with an easier gear. It also gave some of the crew time for a much needed break. As tiring as this race is for the racers, it is equally tiring for the crew. When they are not in direct support, they are taking care of such things as resupply, refueling, washing clothes, and trying to sleep. Those in direct support in the follow car are trying to stay focused mostly traveling at the speed of a man on a bicycle. I did not want a repeat of my previous race when I was hit from behind by the follow car when the driver fell asleep.

As difficult as this section of the race is, it is equally beautiful. It is in stark contrast to the scenery in the desert. From Prescott to Flagstaff, there are miles of national forest, and unusual geological formations. One section is known as the "Arizona Century". It is 100 miles with almost 10,000 feet of climbing. In the middle of this stretch, the race route goes through the quaint little town of Jerome. I always seem to pass through here during happy hour! It can be somewhat torturous to ride through town, and see all the people relaxing with their drinks at the various watering holes on Main Street. I just try to imagine the end of the race, when we'll be doing the same thing in Annapolis.

While making our way through this difficult section, we are once more looking forward to our next race milestone of "Monument Valley". This marks our next desert section, but this time at elevation. This also marks our exit from Arizona into Utah. Just as the desert floor revealed itself at the top of the Glass Elevator, you crest one final hill, and Monument Valley unveils itself in all its glory. Visibility is unlimited, and the view is spectacular. Monolithic rock formations rise straight up from the desert floor, resembling Gods stationed there to look over the Navajo nation. At night, under a full moon, the experience is even more epic. During this section, Maria Parker and her crew made an appearance, and provided much needed inspiration. This was riding session number three. Even though we were nearly 700 miles into the race at this point, I found myself easily able to maintain a speed of around 22 mph on the flat roads.

Unfortunately, the roads are not all flat. Just before Mexican Hat, and yes, there is a rock formation that resembles a sombrero, the terrain starts to undulate once again. This time with even more urgency. Just before the San Juan River, there is one descent of 10%. Here the scenery changes once again as we leave the high desert. Wildlife is now more prevalent, with constant sightings of elk, rabbits and coyotes. At one point, I was nearly taken out, as a Jackrabbit bound across the road as I rode by, passing between my front and rear wheel. Close call, once again riding our wave of good fortune, after our initial stretch of bad luck. We were at this point, focused on our next goal of Durango, at mile 1000. Unfortunately, there is a lot of climbing between here and there. All you can do is take them one at a time.

It will be nice to get out of Utah. It's a nice state, but in addition to the hills, they seem to have placed a low priority on paving roads. In fact, there was one 8 mile section not even paved at all. Just pea gravel. It made for some sketchy descents as the gradients were up to 10%. As I tried to utilize my dormant mountain biking skills, I'm sure I terrified my follow crew as I bombed downhill, glancing to either side seeing the marks in the dirt of other racers who had wiped out before me. Only one thought, keep it going straight! One last lung busting climb, and we were in Colorado. While happy to be here, Colorado meant only one thing, mountains. We had been given a preview already with a couple of peaks of over 7000 feet, but they would pale by comparison to those awaiting us in the Rocky Mountains.

As we took a breather in Cortez, Colorado, we were able to chat with other racers and crews resting there, including those in RAW. With the earlier addition of nearly 100 miles to the race route, it became evident that many were worried about making it to Durango in time. Some crews were nervously monitoring their racer's progress as they had not yet even reached Cortez. This stop proved additionally beneficial to me in that one crew member awaiting the arrival of their racer, was a message therapist, and graciously agreed to provide me with a much needed massage. We were still trying to compensate for the loss of Jim Merchant, our message therapist, who had the unfortunate accident on his way to California.

Thus far in the race, nearly 1000 miles in, we had climbed thousands of feet, gone from sea level to now over 6000 feet in elevation, seen temperatures range from triple digits to the pleasant mid sixties now, and endured a range of humidity changes. One of the side effects of these changing conditions to the human body was the accumulation of fluid, known as "edema". It causes the extremities to swell to sometimes twice their normal size. The flushing of this fluid was one of the major benefits of massage. Sleep deprivation was now also very real for the racers, and caffeine was our friend. The racer for whom my borrowed message therapist was crewing, was struggling to get to Cortez as a result, so we were able to give them a small bottle of spray caffeine we had brought with us in exchange for their gratitude. This was a topical caffeine spray application I had heard about shortly before the race start. Just prior to leaving Cortez, my crew informed me that Joseph had arranged for hotel rooms in Durango for a proper nap. Again, it's the small things. The thought of sleeping in a real bed after four days was the inspiration I needed as I rolled out of Cortez, having said our goodbyes, and wishing well to our new found partners in pain.

By this time in the race, the body is in survival mode. Every bit of energy is being utilized to turn the pedals. As a result, there is none to spare for activities such as keeping the body warm. Even though the temperature was in the mid fifties, I was freezing cold. Several times I stopped the car on the way into Durango to get more clothes to put on, since I was uncontrollably shivering on the descents. I even had to borrow some from the crew, as I did not have enough. The arrival into Durango is one I remember from races past. I even remembered all the turns. As usual, inspired by it being a major milestone in the race, adrenaline kicks in, making the final few miles to time station number 15, situated in scenic Santa Rita Park, along the Animas River, seem effortless. It was here where, if you or your crew have accrued any time penalties for rule infractions along the way, they must be served out in the "penalty box". The benefit of having a well oiled machine as a crew, was that there were no time penalties, so next stop – bed!

THE HARDEST SESSION

Dawn broke in Durango, filling the thin clear air with brilliant sunshine, and myself and the crew with renewed energy and optimism. This marked the 1/3 point in the race. It would have been easy to become complacent at this point, but we knew we still had a long way to go, and were, in fact, still behind schedule. Joseph allowed us to take our well deserved mental vacation, then gently brought us back to reality with the plan for the day. Having discussed our current situation with Maria, it was decided that we needed to produce the most epic day I will have ever had on the bike. That included covering nearly 300 miles, climbing nearly 20,000 feet, while crossing four major mountain passes, three of which topped ten thousand feet. It was good that we had gotten a good rest in Durango. Short, but still good.

We had a sense that this would be a good day, when, as we paused at the side of the road to make a clothing adjustment, Ryan happened to look down by the car and found a short cord that plugged into a special type of phone case. It happened to be the replacement we needed for the one we had that had malfunctioned! I was now able, again, to utilize the phone case/battery pack I had brought specifically for the race. Another crew may have dropped it there, but at any rate, we had what we needed. The Bluetooth communication system was still finicky, but at least now I had a phone for where there was coverage. Our good fortune was only somewhat dampened by the heavy traffic leading out of Durango onto the climb of our first obstacle of the day, Baldy Mountain.

At 7800 feet, Baldy Mountain was just the appetizer for the main course, Wolfcreek Pass. Despite the obvious difficulty of these climbs, it was mitigated by the fact that this was perhaps the most visually stunning part of RAAM. This section is also constantly flanked by rushing streams, so the noise is soothing as well. It is a pleasant break from traffic noise, which is a constant distraction in RAAM. Since the route across the country is as often as possible on secondary highways, cars and trucks pass really close, and the noise is, at times, deafening. You don't realize how fatiguing this can be until late in the race, when you are at the limit as it is. Earplugs would not be a bad idea. I listen to music in my right ear, so that helps a little. For safety reasons, race rules prohibit having an ear bud in the left ear.

Even before crossing Baldy Mountain, we could see snow capped Wolfcreek Pass looming in the distance. It is hard to believe that in the middle of June, there is still snow at those elevations. We would see it firsthand soon enough. The road leading into the start of Wolfcreek pass is painfully slow. It seems to go on forever, and the traffic is heavy. At this point, we only want to get started on the climb. Of course, halfway up the climb, we are longing for the gentler slopes of the lead in. Once on the actual climb, it is nothing but switchbacks all the way to the top. The gradient can hit 20% on the switches, making me thankful Adam was able to find easier gears for my bike. Being the iconic climb on RAAM, it is not surprising that this is where spectators gather to watch the suffering. Since I was riding at a measured pace, it afforded an extended opportunity for viewing. Maria and her crew were there as well, but to offer inspiration. Having ridden this pass herself she knew what it was like. She could always be seen just ahead doing "jumping jacks", and yelling encouragement. At one point, she decided to run alongside me singing songs. Not easy, given the energy required to do so, and the lack of oxygen at that altitude with which to work. She knew what was in store for me on that day, and wanted to do what she could to make it easier.

As we got near the top, the views were spectacular. The streams were full of water from melted snow, and one could look behind, and see the road snake back down into the valley where we started. It seemed to go on forever. It was here, with snow still on the ground, that the crew was able to have a little snowball fight. It was also here, in a previous race, where I made the mistake that cost me the finish. In that race, after this difficult climb, I neglected to put on any warm clothes for the long chilly descent. As a result, my muscles tightened up, and on the next climb after the long descent I strained a quadriceps muscle. I would not make that mistake twice. We stopped at the very top for a photo op, and for me to don more clothes. Additionally, I made it a point to keep my legs moving in the descent in order to keep the blood flowing.

The descent off of Wolfcreek Pass is as epic as the climb up. Unlike the ascent, there were fewer switchbacks, making it possible to attain frightening speed. With tunnels, and slower vehicular traffic, caution was in order. Even so, I found myself passing several cars on my way down. Even after the long descent, we were still at 7500 feet. Without adequate massage, this is when the edema (fluid accumulation in the belly and extremities) became an issue. What I didn't know, was that Jacob had taken the opportunity in the first days of the race to become a "YouTube" expert on the art of massage. That new found skill proved instrumental in keeping me on the bike. One more example of the crew's mantra of improvising for success! This mantra would play out many more times before the race was over.

Next on the day's menu was La Veta Pass. Although nearly as high as Wolfcreek Pass, La Veta Pass is longer and more gradual. Probably a good thing after what we just did. We had now crossed the Continental Divide, another RAAM milestone. The topography was noticeably different now. The climbs were more gradual, and vegetation was thicker and greener. It was dark when we crested La Veta pass and made our way into the valley in the town of La Veta.

Night time is a special time in RAAM. There is less traffic, so it's quieter, and the wildlife is more plentiful. Since I wear a light on my helmet, I am able to look to the sides of the roads and see more of this wildlife. I enjoy riding at night. The time station in La Veta was so vivid in my memory from previous races, I could recall my conversations with my former crew chief, Steve Lufkin, and the welcome cup of hot chocolate he had waiting for me there. I had a cup on that night as well, in his honor. I also remembered the upcoming final pass of this brutal session, Cuchura Pass, and how it was, perhaps the most difficult of the four of this "day's" climbs, especially given what all had just come before. The run up to the final big climb of the Rockies is punctuated by a few welcome flat sections. It seems totally out of place with the dominant terrain. It was on one of these flat stretches when my son, Jesse, rolled up beside me and asked me what time it was. I couldn't see what difference it made, but I looked down at my watch, and told him, "Just after midnight, why?". To which he replied, with a huge grin on his face, "Happy Father's Day!" It was in fact June 19th. That sincere gesture provided me with even more inspiration to do whatever it was going to take to make it to the finish.

As we slowly made our way to the final pass of the Rockies, the sky started to lighten with the first traces of a false dawn. As the features of the landscape started to take shape, we could see lights being turned on in the scattered homes in the area. Dogs started barking at the new day, and the birds started their raucous routine. This section warms up with short steep climbs leading up to the last few miles where the road turns noticeably steeper, with switchbacks more typical of the western Rockies. I kept checking the elevation on my Garmin computer to get an idea of when I might be near the top. I was sure that it was just around the next turn. I was wrong at least ten times before being rewarded with the sight of the sign proclaiming "Cuchura Pass, elevation 9936". This marked the end, almost, of my hardest day on a bike. In celebration, I stood under the sign in order for Adam to take my picture. What I didn't realize, was that he was taking video as well, as I launched into an expletive laced tirade proclaiming that this would be the last time I would ever have to climb this beast. This, unfortunately, made it on to Facebook.

Just after the summit is Monument lake. It is a spectacular lake seemingly out of place at the top of a mountain. We took this opportunity to rest for a short spell, and just enjoy the moment. Caught up in that moment, I forgot that I still had another 45 mile to go to get to Trinidad, which would mark the end of this epic session. There were still more rolling hills on the way down, before tracing the Purgatoire River into Trinidad. These hills were teasers in that by building enough momentum on the way down each one, I could almost coast to the top of the next one, but not quite. Once I made my way into the valley, fatigue was really setting in. I had been on the bike now for over 24 hours on this day, 5 days into the race. With all that I could remember about this section from years past, I can't explain why I couldn't recall the final brutal hill leading into town. It was like a slap on my worn out face. Once into town, I gratefully caught sight of the energized crew assembled around the RV. After a quick shower, and some much needed sustenance, I climbed into the back to sleep. Somehow, sleep would not come. In my heightened state of excitement, I could hear every little noise, and the AC in the RV was not cooperating. Add to that the fact that it was windy enough to rock the RV, and what should have been instant sleep came at the expense of valuable time.

YES, TOTO, WE'RE IN KANSAS

Trinidad, Colorado was the last time station before flatter land. Although we were still above 5000 feet, the terrain was a little more forgiving. We will still be above 3000 feet for much of our time in Kansas. Even so, the trend now was down, as we made our way toward the Mississippi River. So far, the wind was cooperating, so we were making good time. It wasn't helping, but it wasn't hurting either. In the past. It had been strong enough to sandblast the paint off of my spokes! Eastern Colorado looks a lot like Kansas. So much so, that at one point, I was told, eastern Colorado tried to secede from the state, and become part of Kansas. As we neared Ulysses, we knew we were entering Kansas, because in the RAAM race book, there is, at this this point, an entire section devoted on how to deal with the potential for tornadoes. Although I have never experience one there, it has happened in years past, so you always have to be prepared. Mention "Kansas" to anyone who has raced RAAM, and you are likely to get the same reaction. It consists of the shaking of the head, and the sucking in of breath. RAAM racers have a love/hate relationship with the state. Although the people are gracious, the wind can be unforgiving, and the scenery uninspiring.

Kansas is significant in several ways. First, and foremost, it marks the midpoint in the race. This is an important psychological boost, as by now, fatigue and saddle sores have set in with a vengeance. This affords us the opportunity to see the light at the end of the tunnel. This year was significant for another reason. We were riding for the charity "3000 Miles to a Cure". The charity already meant a lot to us, but we were starting to realize a phenomenon as a result of our efforts. We were already a curiosity, with our gaudily marked vehicles, flashing lights, and a rider looking like death warmed over, so people naturally asked us about it whenever we stopped. I was amazed by how many people had been personally touched by the insidious disease, brain cancer. I was even more touched by the number of people who, with tears in their eyes, told their story, and donated various amounts of money to the cause. Often all they had, and as little as one dollar, or the change in their pocket. We were all touched by the selfless generosity. Between that, and our on-line efforts at fund raising, by the end of the race,

Rob DeCou's team and mine, had raised more than $40,000 for brain cancer research.

By this point in the race, we had all started to collect stories that help to make this race an enormous part of all of our lives. In addition to the numerous on site donations, the interactions with people as we slowly made our way east restored our faith in mankind. At one point, at around two in the morning, somewhere near Wichita, we stopped briefly at an all night convenience store for supplies, and a short break. As we decompressed in one corner of the parking lot, we were approached by four local police officers. We were not the first RAAM racers to pass by, so they already knew what we were up to, but were curious as to what motivated us. One officer, Nick Piatt, asked if he could ride my bike around the parking lot. He said he had a lunch bet riding on it. I readily agreed, thinking that it would be time I would not have to be on it, and of course, a bet is a bet. I should have told him about the saddle being impregnated with 1500 miles worth of chamois butter. I hope it didn't stain his uniform too badly. It was only upon his return, bet won, that he relayed that, his life too, had been personally touched by brain cancer. When we gave him one of our stickers, he proudly affixed it to the front cover of his citation book. Maybe it was the fatigue, or just the humanity, but it was a very emotional moment. After posing for a group picture, we were once again, off into the stillness of the night.

By now, saddle sores had become a real problem. Prior to the race, I had experimented with several different saddles, looking for the remedy. One in particular, had worked well in the Sebring 24 hour qualifier, so I thought I had it resolved. As a backup, I brought several other saddles, thinking I could rotate them and distribute the pressure unique with each saddle.

I am sure Adam was getting sick of switching saddles on a regular basis. Fortunately, my Eddy Merckx bike had been fault free, so switching saddles, had been his only major task, other than keeping up with his Tinder on line dating account. My only other option, at this point, was to start wearing two sets of bib shorts. One inside out over the other. This actually worked pretty well, but was not perfect. At any rate, we were not going to let saddle sores keep us from getting to Annapolis. All we could do was keep it from becoming infected. That could keep us from our goal. It was at this point in the race, that Tyler assumed a new responsibility. He was now the official "undercarriage inspector". It was his dubious duty to visually inspect my saddle sores to make sure they were not becoming infected. For me, the hard part was the anticipation of how painful the initial sit was going to be after each break. Knowing you were about to plop your entire weight, what was left of it, down upon open sores was not something to be taken lightly.

In the long flat plains of Kansas is where the math started to rear its head. Joseph and Tyler had run the numbers and knew we were behind. At one point, east of Wichita, the follow car pulled up, and Jesse leaned out to tell me of the concern regarding our progress. I was doing the math as well, and was not as concerned, but knowing I was even more fatigued than the rest, I started to doubt my calculations. Joseph and Tyler were both more adept with numbers, so I was in no position to doubt them. In my reduced state, I was also unable to adequately explain my reasoning. I was basing my calculations on my current overall average, which was still good enough to finish in time, but they were using the trend. We were both correct, but the intangible in my mind, that I was unable to convey, was that we had just crossed the Rocky Mountains, so the trend should start to reverse, now that the big bumps were over. After a few back and forths, we were at an impasse, so I just went went back to what I was here for, and that was to ride my bike. I would just have to prove them wrong.

As flat as Kansas is thought of as being, it is far from it. The terrain undulates, and the hills are short and quick. The only consolation is that the trend is "downward". It may be only 500 feet over a span of 80 miles, but we were looking for anything positive, so that worked. Also, the scenery seldom changed, so that led to boredom. It was purely agricultural. Sometimes the only break in the visual monotony, was a large grain silo on the horizon. We could see them from 20 miles away, so it took a long time to even reach each one. Another phenomenon at night at this point, was that with the unrestricted visibility, if there were any other competitors in the area, we could see the flashing yellow lights of their follow vehicles from miles away. By now, the teams had not yet caught up to us, so we knew that everyone was a solo racer. Since we were now well into the race, and fatigue was a factor for everyone, breaks for all were frequent, albeit short. As a result, sometimes we would pass, and other times, we would be passed. There was a certain bond at this point between all the teams, and it was not so much a competition, as it was everyone wishing the best for each other. If anyone needed anything, other teams were happy to provide it. Occasionally, riders would ride alongside each other, although the rules were strict about how long you could do so. During those times, we would ask how the other was doing, how was the body holding up, and if anyone had found a cure for saddle sores. It was from one of those conversations in my previous race, that I discovered Ambesol from a fellow racer. Meant for easing teething pain in the gums of infants, it also worked well on open sores on one's backside. It didn't fix it, but it numbed it, so you could forget about it for a while. I was happy to disseminate that valuable piece if information to my fellow competitors in need, and if we had extra, offer some.

Somewhere near the halfway point, approaching Pratt, Kansas, Maria and her entourage caught up with us again. With the dawn of each day, spirits naturally rose, and with our closing in on the halfway point, they rose even more. One of the ways I pass time on the long monotonous stages of the race, besides listening to my music through one ear, was to crack jokes. Unfortunately, they were almost always in the form on puns. If I had to suffer, so did everyone else. I remember one stretch of road, while passing endless fields of livestock, engaging in an exchange with the media crew that must have lasted for over an hour. Every time they would pull up alongside, I would have another pun ready for them, and whenever possible, them for me.

"Why do cows have bells around their necks? Because their horns don't work."

"I wouldn't 'steer' you wrong."

"That's a bunch of bull!"
"You're 'udderly' ridiculous."

"Be careful at that intersection. I wouldn't want you to get "T-boned".

"What's your beef?"

"Hey Marshall, how does your butt feel?"

"Like ground chuck."

NEXT STOP, THE MISSISSIPPI

The halfway point in this race, is
exciting and depressing at the same time.
While it meant that we had covered 1500
miles, it meant that we had 1500 more to go!
No one knows where the exact halfway point
is, and with our additional miles this year, it
was even more of an unknown. Nevertheless, it
didn't stop some crews from marking their best
guess of that point by painting a line on the
road for their rider to see, and the crew to
celebrate. As a result, there were about a
dozen "best guesses", and corresponding lines
on the road. Oh well, I guess we'll just
celebrate each time to be sure, and work on an
average.

Kansas, as a state, made it a point to give us a proper undulating send off, and to give us a preview of what was awaiting us in Missouri. The hills from Maize all the way to Fort Scott were short and punchy. Only two to three hundred feet each, they were not large hills, but the frequency took its toll on an already stressed body. This was just a preview of what was to come in Missouri. Missouri is home to the Ozark Mountains. They are like the love child of the Rockies, and the Appalachians. Although not as famous as the two other big ranges, they deserve respect just the same. There is a mix of climbs, ranging from short and steep, to long and gradual. It is hard to find a rhythm. Much depends on the route. Much of this part of the race goes back and forth across the Missouri river. Close to the river, in the flood plain, it is pan flat, but just a mile or so from the river, the climbs are brutal. As around any large river, the population is much denser. This means that the traffic is much worse as well. America has yet to embrace the bicycle as the efficient mode of transportation it is, and as a result, the roads are built for cars alone. Depending upon the time of day, people are trying to get either to or from work. A bicycle is just in the way. Add to that a slow moving follow vehicle, and patience can grow thin.

This was our situation in Missouri. Steep hills and thick traffic. The rules of RAAM dictate that whenever a rider and crew are slowing traffic, we are required to pull off the road, and let the traffic pass. On these roads, this is not always easy. There are few places to pull over, and if on a steep hill, it is difficult and frustrating to get moving again form a dead stop. These areas became just a section to survive. In years past, I can recall times when frustrated drivers would, after having been slowed down, speed past us honking and yelling. There are many diesel pick up trucks in this area, and they had a technique of stepping on the gas as they passed, spewing a cloud of thick black diesel exhaust, leaving me chewing on a soot sandwich. For some reason, this year was different. I was pleasantly surprised when, instead of the usual vitriol, I was greeted with shouted words of encouragement as drivers went past. Between that, and the inherent beauty of the state, it made this part of the race much more pleasant than in years past.

One of the most beautiful areas of Missouri is just before Camdenton. After a brutal section of ups and downs, we climbed one last steep hill, and were rewarded with a spectacular view of Lake of the Ozarks. A massive reservoir of the Osage River, like an oasis, it seems totally out of place. It could not have come at a better time. We had been going hard trying to make up time, and I needed a break. The time station was most accommodating with an assortment of food and drink. I gratefully climbed off the bike and made my way into the RV for a couple of hours of much needed sleep. We were seven days into the race, and my sleep total was barely twenty hours. With another tough push to the Mississippi ahead, we did not have the luxury of time to sleep.

BIG MUDDY

After our brief stop in Camdenton, and a much needed resupply of junk food from the nearby all night McDonalds, we began our final push to the Mississippi. Dawn broke as we neared Jefferson City. Even that early, traffic was heavy, and as is often the case, navigation on the RAAM route was difficult.

In one five mile stretch through the heart of downtown, past the capitol, there are multiple, seemingly unnecessary turns. My follow car at that time was being manned by my son, Jesse, and Jacob. One of my few moments of frustration came at a most inopportune time. As I approached an intersection, I was unsure of my next turn, and so were they. Instead of pulling over to figure it out, I yelled for them to tell me which way to go. Being as invested in this race as I, and not wanting to make a mistake, they were unable to reach a consensus between them. Things became heated, and each of them being intense individuals, nearly came to blows. Seeing that, and realizing that it was totally my fault, I stopped and we slowly deescalated the situation. We finally got our bearings and proceeded along the correct route, but a rift had formed between them, and Joseph was forced to make some crew changes as a result.

Missouri was not going to give up without a fight, and that was proven in the last 150 miles leading us to the Mississippi River. Steep and relentless, it crossed the Missouri river several times, and the bluffs on either side were painfully steep. Add to that fog, and the potential for mishap was great. The winding roads, combined with the fog and fatigue, made it nearly impossible to know whether I was climbing or descending. I was forced to look at my Garmin bike computer to see if the elevation was increasing or decreasing. It was also now the "witching hour" again, that time between two and five a.m. when it was difficult to stay awake, even if one was adequately rested. I remember being forced to take a couple of "combat naps" right on the asphalt on the side of the road. By the time we reached Washington, Missouri, we had covered over 2000 miles, which was more than the total distance of the professional grand tour of Spain, La Vuelta a Espana.

Just past Washington, the route presented us with one last kick in the butt of a climb, before dumping us onto the flood plain of the Mississippi. For the next 35 miles, we would be zigzagging through flat fields of nothing, seemingly at random. If I didn't know better, I would swear they were trying to spell out "R-A-A-M" with the route. This was another section which seemed like a cruel joke by the race officials just to make us suffer. I'm sure there was a more direct route! Add to that the stifling heat, and the humidity from being near the river, and this became a difficult section. In a previous attempt, I had fallen completely asleep on the bike in this section, resting on the aerobars, waking up just in time to keep from crashing. As we mercifully made our last turn on our approach to the Mississippi river, I could see the gas plaza that served as the time station, which marked the second time cutoff for the race. I could also see the RV, but knew that, although we had made the second time cutoff, I would not be afforded the opportunity to utilize it for sleep. We had little time to celebrate. We still had more than 900 of the toughest miles to go. At least now we could say that we had covered more miles that both the 2016 Il Giro d'Italia, and the 2016 Le Tour de

France.

SADDLE SORES AND BUMPY ROADS

Once back on the bike on my way over the Mississippi River, we were now in Illinois. Another welcome milestone. An unwelcome milestone, however, was the severity of my saddle sores. None of our tricks were working. Adam was probably sick of swapping saddles, as I desperately tried to find one that would offer some small measure of relief. I was not going to let that be the thing that caused us to fail, so I was forced to just press on. It did not help that, one section was so rough, that we were forced to stop and let as much air out of my tires as we dared in an effort to cushion the ride without causing a pinch flat. A pinch flat being when the bumps are so bad that the tire bottoms out on the rim with impact, pinching the tube, and causing a puncture. This short section was a real low point. Joseph and Tyler were forced to calm me down, as I was ready to toss my bike into the adjacent field, and call it quits, all the while cursing the race directors for going out of their way to find this horrendous piece of rutted asphalt that passed as a road. I know in London, they ride on the left of the road. Here, we rode on what was left of the road!

As we crept along this brutal stretch of road, and I use the term loosely, we finally crested a small rise, and saw the right hand turn that would finally put us on smooth road. I'll never know if this stretch was put in deliberately just to make this nearly impossible race even harder, but it served to cement our resolve. We decided that there was nothing they could do stop us. It was a good thing, too, because they were not done yet. Another unique aspect of this race, was how tightly bunched competitors can become. It was amazing that, this far into the race, we were playing leapfrog with several other racers. It was nice to briefly chat, and take solace in the fact that, everyone was suffering. At this point, the suffering had become too great for many, and they had been forced to abandon. For others, including myself, the realization of not making the time cutoff was also looming.

It was in the rolling hills of Illinois, as we made our way to Indiana, that I had my first experience with hallucinations. I didn't see things, but in my mind I was somewhere other than in the race. At one point, I was on a Saturday morning group ride with an unfamiliar, but friendly, group. They were describing the route to me as we made one of the long slow climbs. When the follow car pulled alongside near the top, it took me a minute to even recognize Ryan Jean, who had been a constant presence since the beginning of the race. Once I realized who he was, I seemed to snap back to reality. Unfortunately, I never got to say goodbye to my imaginary friends with whom I had been riding. I'm pretty sure I won the imaginary sprint.

The short mental vacation seemed to rejuvenate me for a while, as we made quick work of Illinois. Although lumpy towards the end, the promise of a new state line propelled us forward. In addition to crossing into Indiana, over the Wabash River, we were now in the Eastern time zone. This was "race time", and a huge milestone. From the beginning of the race, all times had been predicated on Eastern Daylight Time, since that is what it would be at the finish. This is done to avoid confusion when calling in arrival times as we checked in at each time station. At this point, the time stations themselves served as mini goals. Spaced approximately fifty miles apart, each one passed, was that much closer to the end!

It was now a matter of grinding to the finish. We were confident in the plan that Joseph and Tyler had plotted out, the crew pairings were working well, and I was feeling strong. Fatigue and saddle sores were still factors, but it seemed as though I had during the last 2300 miles ridden myself into even better shape. We were now nearing Ohio, where Adam was from, having just graduated from college. His family lived there, and he was looking forward to seeing them. They promised a good meal for the crew, so we were looking forward to it as well. The next 200 miles, although hilly as usual, was punctuated by several scenic parks, and college towns. We also passed through the quaint village of Oldenburg, with classic German style housed, and even road signs in German (as well as English, thank goodness!).

Shortly after passing Oldenburg, we made it to Oxford, Ohio. Another state, but more importantly, Adam Darby's home town. As promised, there was a welcome meal waiting for us, hot showers, and one last pleasant surprise. Adam's sister gifted us with an assortment of local ice cream. During a race like this, the body goes through several dietary phases. Cravings based on what the body knows it needs. At first I was craving carbohydrates, since I was fresh, and riding in the zone that utilizes that. Later, I craved protein, as I had settled in, and was metabolizing fat for fuel. If fat depletes, the body will start burning its own muscle protein in order to make fuel. It is possible, in this condition to overload the kidneys with so much protein to metabolize, that there is a risk of going into renal failure. Obviously, not a good thing. I had by this point, without even sensing it, used up most of my fat stores. I knew I was craving something, but did not know what. It must have been fat, because the ice cream was the answer! We also took this opportunity for me to take a much needed sleep break. While I slept, Joseph planned out our strategy for the rest of the race.

THE CALM BEFORE THE STORM

Refreshed from our break in Oxford, we optimistically pressed on. We were now 600 miles from the finish. We were rested, and on schedule. Unfortunately, we had forgotten those sage words of Mike Tyson, the boxer, regarding "plans", and "punches". Our "punch in the face" came just after Blanchester, Ohio. Blanchester was vividly and painfully etched in my memory. It was shortly after there where my first RAAM effort had ended in 2011. The time station after Blanchester was Chillicothe. That was as far as I had made it. Our lives almost ended there as well, when as we dejectedly drove away in defeat, our driver fell asleep, and we narrowly avoided a head on collision. Shortly after Blanchester, near the small town of New Vienna, our race nearly ended once again.

I had experience fatigue before in this race, but nothing like what hit me on this night. Although only 100 miles from my last break, the urge to sleep suddenly hit me like an avalanche. It buried me, and I could not keep my head above the smothering waves of total exhaustion. We had already been utilizing every caffeine product known to man, including a topical spray, as well as vitamin B-12, Red Bull, and 5 Hour Energy. Tonight, nothing was working at all. I kept telling Joseph, who was in the follow car at the time, that my legs felt strong, but I just couldn't keep my eyes open! I was barely making forward progress, and was dangerously weaving all over the road. Fortunately, it was the middle of the night, with very little traffic. My final strategy to cope with this debilitating condition, was to pull over, and take one of my "combat naps". Hopefully, one REM cycle of sleep, lasting about 15 minutes, would rejuvenate me, and I would be able to continue. It had worked thus far, so we were optimistic that it would work again.

HAIL MARY

We pulled over in the parking lot of the
Clinton-Highland joint fire station, and I fell
asleep as soon as my helmeted head hit the
pavement. The crew was helpless, as all they
could do was wait, sure that I would pop up
and once again, charge down the road after my

15 minutes of sleep. Fifteen minutes went by, and I didn't stir. Ten more minutes, and still nothing. Tyler finally took the risk of trying to wake me, but to no avail. At this point, they knew that the short nap was not going to do it. I had completely shut down from fatigue. Alarm bells were ringing in Joseph's head, as this was definitely not in the plan. Our success was predicated, at this point, on sticking to a tight schedule to ensure completion of the race. Joseph and Tyler were forced to recalculate the remainder of our race to try and determine if it was still possible to finish on time, given this new wrinkle. Joseph remembered that I was telling him that my legs were strong, so he weighed that into what had to be the riskiest decision he had to make the entire race. He was faced with two options. Force me up and on the bike, and hope that somehow I would miraculously recover, or take the huge chance of letting me sleep for an extended period, and

hope for the equally miraculous possibility that I could wake up, and cover the last 500 miles non-stop in 50 hours.

After careful calculations, and reviewing my performance up to this point, Joseph opted for the "Hail Mary". As I lay passed out on the asphalt, Joseph contacted the RV, and called them back to New Vienna, where we had stopped. The first I was aware of any of this, was when Tyler tried to get me to stand. I could not. Tyler and Joseph then proceeded to carry me onto the RV, and deposit me on the bed, where I resumed my catatonic state. As the clock ticked, Joseph and Tyler were busy calculating an alternate plan to salvage the race. I awoke after about four hours, but was told to go back to sleep. It was now all or nothing. Finally, after two more blissful hours, I woke up again, sensed the bustling activity, and knew it was time to put up, or shut up.

Thankfully, everyone was calm, having agreed with the decision, and determining that it was the only viable option. That kept me calm, and focused on the task at hand. More determined than ever, as were they. As I scarfed down some quick food, and got ready to ride, I was pleasantly surprised at how fresh I felt. It was not time to think of what lay ahead for us. In fact, I wanted to ride, so I wouldn't think about it. I'm sure everyone on the crew was worried, but none of them showed it. We were a team, and we had one goal; Annapolis, Maryland.

Back on the bike and down the road I pedaled. Next stop, Athens, Ohio.

Athens, Ohio is home to the University of Miami, Ohio. It is a beautiful campus, and the race directors were determined that we see all of it. All well and good, except that many of the streets are paved in bricks, and bricks are not smooth. An even more poignant reminder of my saddle sores. Throughout the race, the teams are required to remain in daily contact with the race directors. This is to enable crews to be updated on changing conditions. This included this year, a section we were forced to bypass because of reports of a vicious dog. On this day, as we wound our way through the campus, we received another such instruction. We were informed via text message of a route change. The change involved making an unscheduled turn before proceeding back on course. All well and good, if it were not for the fact that the original text included the instruction: "Turn left, onto an unmarked alley", when in fact, the turn was to the right. We became hopelessly lost, but finally managed to find our way to the next time station, although not by the prescribed route. This was going to result in the loss of even more valuable time.

Race rules mandate that the route be followed to the letter. Every turn, including the revised ones. Due to the mis-typed text, we had not followed the course in its entirety. Although the text had been subsequently amended, we had not gotten it in time. The only solution for this, even though it was not our mistake, was to go back to the point of our missed turn, and for me to re-ride the course correctly. Although this meant losing more time we did not have, it was the only option in order for us to do to maintain the integrity of our race. To add insult to injury (literally), the revised section contained even more cobblestone. All we could do was follow our mantra of overcoming all obstacles. As we reassembled in the parking lot of the mall that served as the time station in Athens, after rectifying our navigational error, we saw a race official who had been observing our actions. He told us we had done exactly what we should have done, so our moral decision was even further validated.

WELCOME TO WEST VIRGINIA

The next time station after Athens, Ohio is West Union, West Virginia. Not only is it one of the longest at 86 miles away, it also leads us to the foothills of the Appalachian Mountains. I remembered this section from my last race, when it took me over ten hours to complete, and was the beginning of the end for us that year. Fresh from my extended rest, and still feeling strong, I was flying now. It seemed like a different route all together from my recollection of the first time. Even though I felt as though I was going fast, I knew from experience, that reality was sometimes different from perception. I can remember often thinking I must be going over 20 mph, and upon looking at my speedometer, see that I was going much slower. At one point during this stretch this year, I felt really slow, so actually asked the follow car to look and see if maybe I had a flat tire. I was relieved to find out that, in fact, I did! The failure of our radios did have an unexpected benefit that would prove useful towards the end of the race. Not only had we worked out hand signals for the passing of the various drinks I was utilizing, but we had developed a horn system for navigation. When we came to a turn, the follow car would signal the correct direction with horn honks. One honk meant left, two meant right, and three meant straight ahead. It was alphabetical, so that made it easier. As long as I remembered the alphabet. It also helped keep me awake, and the crew aware of my mental state. I was required to acknowledge the direction with a "thumbs up", so as long as I did that, and turned the correct way, all was good. At times, we were all anxious for a turn, just to make sure we were good.

We were now approaching the point at which my second race had ended. I vividly remembered each turn and climb leading up to that point. I did not know if I was going to complete the race this year, but I now knew that I was going to make it farther than I ever had. That knowledge gave me a much needed boost.

Much of this part of the route uses State Road 50, usually the business route. With Joseph and Tyler in the follow car, I rounded a bend, started a descent, looked over, and saw the exact spot where we had called it quits in my last race. A small florist shop on the right hand side of the road. As I rode past, I looked over and emphatically gestured with our symbolic salute, usually reserved for crossing state lines. Not knowing what I was doing, Joseph pulled alongside to ask. As I explained, I could feel the determination strengthen even more. I'm sure theirs did as well. Joseph and Tyler, as well as Jesse, Adam, Ryan, and Jacob had selflessly signed on for my foolish adventure, and had sacrificed more than two weeks of their lives, not to mention time away from their families. I was going to do everything within my power to hold up my end of the bargain. 300 miles to the finish.

We were now in the heart of the Appalachians. After ten days on the bike, these already substantial mountains seemed even larger. This, however, was the type of mountains I had trained on for this race. As a result, I was familiar with the unique gradients of the climbs, so the difficulty was somewhat mitigated. This was also virgin territory for me, and therefore exciting. I could almost taste my finisher's Stella! That was not to say it would be easy. I still had to make it to the finish without another sleep break. To alleviate some of the boredom, Jacob had devised a clever tactic to help. On the bike, there was a tiny canvas cargo box on the top tube, called a "bento box", used to store small supplies that I could easily reach. At each time station, Jacob had taken to filling the bento box with various treats. Candy, gum, small cookies, whatever he could find. I would leave each time station, and wait as long as I could to see what was inside. I was like a kid at Christmas, anxious to open his presents.

This tactic was nearly perfect, except that it did not take into account the mischievous nature of some of the crew. This far into the race, with fatigue firmly entrenched in all of us, core personality traits came to the surface. Joseph and Tyler compensated for their fatigue by resorting to their analytical nature. An accountant and an engineer, they were constantly crunching the numbers. Ryan, devoted adventurer, had turned this into one big epic adventure. He did all the cooking and slept outside in his tent whenever he could. He did learn on the first night, however, that if you were in the desert, and pitched your tent in a patch of green grass, odds are, the grass didn't stay that green without some help. Sort of like finding a turtle on a fence post. No sooner had he crawled inside his tent, than the sprinklers timed on, directing the full force of the water into his tent. Lesson learned. Jesse and Adam were perhaps the most laid back. Constantly cracking jokes, they kept the mood light. The more tired they got, the funnier they became. Considering how haphazardly these six individuals had been thrown together, it was nothing short of a miracle how efficient they all were as a team. It was going to take every bit of this efficiency to give us any hope of success.

THINGS THAT GO BANG IN THE NIGHT

As we made our way through West Virginia, darkness once again descended upon us. This was as usual, a tough time to stay awake, let alone alert. Fortunately, this night would be a little easier. At around 2am, we came up on an individual on the side of the road, in the middle of nowhere, frantically waving his arms. When we asked what was wrong, he said, "I think I've had a heart attack!" He wanted us to take him to the hospital. He was a young man, and quite active, so Jesse and Ryan decided that a heart attack was unlikely. More believable was a pharmaceutical reaction (drugs). We could not afford to stop anyway, so we offered the use of a phone so he could call someone he knew in order to pick him up. Onward we pressed. This bit of excitement allowed me to delay the opening of my bento box for a little longer, but soon, I couldn't stand it, and had to find out what treats Jacob had for me tonight. What I didn't know was that Jacob was not the only one who had a hand in preparing my treats. As I reached in, I could feel the usual assortment of gum and cookies, but also new unidentifiable objects. I figured it must be a new candy, so I was eager to try one. I placed one in my mouth, but could not tell what it was from the texture. I thought maybe it was a hard candy, so I bit into it. Instead of the tart sugary taste I was expecting, there was instead, the taste of gunpowder, accompanied by a small explosion! It was a firecracker. Called a "Pop Rock", it was designed to be thrown on the ground and explode upon impact. Fully awake now, I drifted back to find out what exactly they were thinking when they put them in my treat box.

"Did you do that on purpose?", I asked.

Ryan replied, "We thought you would know what they were, and throw them at us for a little excitement."

I asked, "Did it not occur to you that someone going on ten days with very little sleep, might decide to eat it?"

Ryan replied, "Well yes, we thought of that, so we made sure it was safe, just in case."

"How exactly did you do that?" I asked, to which Ryan replied, "Jesse and I each bit one to make sure it wouldn't hurt!"

At this point, all I could do was laugh....and throw the remaining Pop Rocks at them.

CASUALTIES

The attrition rate for solo racers in RAAM is brutal. Each year is different, but usually in excess of 50%. Some develop problems early and are forced to drop out almost before they even get started, and others make it nearly to the end, such as myself in two previous attempts. Going out early may be the more merciful way to DNF (did not finish), because making it so close without finishing is just cruel. You have suffered as much as any finisher, but have nothing to show for it.

One year, a racer made it to the last time station before having to drop out. Sometimes problems develop early, and the rider wills himself to continue, hoping for a miracle. As I rode from Grafton towards our next goal of Maryland, I came upon one such brave soul. As I neared, I could see the tell tale signs of his Shermer's Neck (a condition when the neck muscles are unable to keep one's head up). I could see the fabricated neck brace his crew had constructed for him. A bulky collection of straps and PVC pipe, it was the only thing keeping his head upright. He could not turn his head, so was forced to stare straight ahead. His pace was slowing and I sadly realized that he was probably not going to make it to the finish. He probably knew it as well, but was willing himself on, refusing to quit. It's that kind of extraordinary spirit that makes this race even more special. I spoke with him for our allotted 15 minutes, wished him well, and pressed on alone, strangely thankful for suffering only from fatigue and saddle sores. I had been that casualty twice before, and did not want to make it three.

In a cruel twist, the next time station after Grafton, West Virginia, is actually in the state of Maryland. Maryland is where we eventually finish, but not before first dipping south into Pennsylvania, before once again entering Maryland for the last time. This is also an extremely hilly section. In one ironic twist, we were once again required to climb Wolf Creek. The first one was in Colorado, this one in West Virginia, and almost as steep. It had a gradient of 8%, but thankfully is only 3 miles long. Five miles after that, we were in the state of Maryland, with "only" 275 miles to go, and 24 hours to get there. As I rolled into the beautiful town of McHenry, and stopped at the time station across from a scenic lake, I thought to myself, "What a great place to take a long break." If only I could. I was still 266 miles from the finish, running out of time, and on fumes.

The next 50 miles would be the calm before the storm. A relatively benign section, it did not prepare us for the last gut shot to our efforts, in the form of some really steep climbs. The climbs between Cumberland and Hancock, Maryland are notoriously difficult. So much so, that the five consecutive climbs have acquired the nickname of "The Five Bitches". Although they lived up to their reputation, perhaps because of the anticipation, I did not find them to be as difficult as I thought they would be. What I didn't know, was that the next climb, that nobody mentioned, was a beast! Totally unexpected. Although short, it was the steepest of the race. I can remember feeling sorry for myself at this point, and having my first real crisis of confidence. I was tired, sore, sleepy, and wondering what the hell I was thinking when I entered this race for the third time. At this point the encouragement of my crew was what kept me on the bike. This was where it was truly apparent just what a team effort this race is.

The race organizers must have somehow known that this was a crucial point for the racers and their crews, so they must have routed this part of the course for a little extra motivation. They never did seem to take the easy way to anywhere, always seeming to find the worst roads for us to travel on. From the dirt roads in Utah, the potholes in Indiana, to the cobbles in Ohio, they managed to find the worst of our nation's highways and biways. The circuitous route on this night, however, so close to the finish, was the exception. As we descended the last of the brutal climbs in this race, instead of going straight, which would have been the more direct route, we took a left onto Pumping Station Road. What came next made this deviation the most memorable of the race, as we entered Gettysburg National Historical Park. In the misty darkness, with thousands of fireflies blinking in the still air on both sides of us, we passed the ancient caissons silently standing guard over this iconic battlefield of America's Civil War. When I thought of the thousands who lost their lives in this bloody battle, my minor complaints seemed all the more insignificant. Those who gave their lives for this cause, much like those for whom we were racing, who were fighting brain cancer, had not chosen their misery, as had I. I was humbled and ashamed. I was also motivated more than ever to finish this race. So many people had donated money, and sent words of encouragement, we were no longer racing for ourselves, we were racing for them.

PUSH TO THE FINISH

We were now under 100 miles to go! This would, however, prove to be the hardest 100 miles of the race. We had been racing for 11 days, and 3000 miles. Adrenaline, and the finish line was all that kept me on the bike. Much of this last part is a blur to me, and had to be reconstructed for me by the crew. I was in a dream state. I remember seeing Karl Koops, an old college soccer team mate at one time station, but I'm not sure which one. I do remember him offering me a beer, which, as much as I wanted to accept, could not yet do so. He promised to save it for me at the finish line. This is also where I lost two of my crew. Joseph and Tyler had used up there allotted time, and had to leave to go catch their flights home. I only vaguely remember that discussion. The good news was that we were able to pick up replacement crew members from Rob's crew, since he had just finished his race a few hours earlier. Brothers Chris and Tyler Clemens stepped in and saved our race. Otherwise, we would have been forced to try to finish with just four crewmen, an obstacle we may not have been able to overcome at this late stage. I remember seeing them at the next time station, and thinking that they had been with us the whole time. Reality was now blending with fantasy. It would only get worse.

Another night, and while it would be our last, it did not mitigate the problem of staying awake. Adding to the difficulty was that we were on a long straight road. Jacob went on to the internet with his phone to a website featuring a collection of really bad jokes. He tortured me with them in order to help me keep my eyes open. This got us to the last time station in Pennsylvania, Hanover. From here, it was back into Maryland, and the finish. With the passing of each time station, I would ask for a status check. "What average do I need to maintain in order to finish on time?" Each time, the number got smaller. "You need to average 14", ".....13", ".....12." This meant that as long as I maintained a speed above that average, and we had not accrued any time penalties to be served at the Mt. Airy time station, we would finish before the cut off. What I didn't know, was that before Joseph and Tyler left, they wisely padded the calculations to give us a buffer, in case something went wrong. What could possibly go wrong?

Leaving Hanover, I had a crew change. The return of Ryan and my son Jesse, of "pop rock" fame. The approach into Mt. Airy consists of more long straight roads, with rolling hills. Here is where my mind started its early vacation.

As I made my way along the route, I was fine (relatively) physically, but mentally out of it. At one point I motioned for the follow car to pull over. When they stopped, I asked Ryan, "Where am I. What am I doing, "and as I looked at the spare bikes on top of the car, "and why am I the only one riding a bike." Ryan very calmly answered, "You are racing in RAAM on your way to Mt. Airy. You are riding solo, so you are the only one allowed on the bike." "But why are we going this way? Isn't there a shorter route?" I asked. An odd question, given that I had never in my life been there before. "This is the route they gave us, and we have to stay on it." was all he said in reply. Satisfied with his answer, I climbed back on the bike and continued on my way. Part of my mind, however, was still not satisfied. For some reason, I thought I was heading for the finish, and was about to be disqualified for missing the time cutoff. Frantic, I rode as fast as I could toward Mt. Airy. After eleven and a half days on the bike, Ryan and Jesse must have thought me insane as I furiously sped along at speeds in excess of 25 mph, attacking each hill out of the saddle. Adding to the bizarre dreamlike state I was in, was the fact that I seemed to know where I was going. Road signs were familiar, and I already seemed to know where each turn was going to be even before I was told. I knew to take the final left turn that would get me to the bike shop that served as time station 52.

Rolling into the bike shop parking lot, still full of adrenaline, I thought that I had made my imaginary time cutoff, and that I was done. I had somehow convinced myself that this was the finish line. It took several minutes of calm, and delicate explanation by the crew to convince me that I still had a little over twenty miles yet to go. I remember being shown the route profile for the last section, and having it pointed out to me that it was all downhill. Well, not exactly, but it did trend that way. Finally convinced, and down from the adrenaline high, with no time penalties to be served, I climbed back onto my bike and started the final leg of our adventure. First to Odenton, then Annapolis. What the profile didn't show was that we would be riding through a busy part of town during rush hour. After everything we had been through, rush hour traffic would be the closest we would come to disaster.

After a few "normal" miles, and as the sun started to peek over the horizon, my mind, maybe as a defense mechanism, started its journey back into fantasy land. Half of me was fully aware of what was going on, so to an outside observer, everything seemed normal. I was coherent, and riding well. What no one could see, was what was going on inside my head. As I encountered thickening rush hour traffic, cars passed closer and closer, seemingly intent in their efforts to send a message to us that they were not happy that we were costing them precious seconds of their commute. I remember the angry glares of drivers as they passed, holding cups of their morning coffee. The entire time this was taking place in reality, an imaginary conversation was taking place in my head. I was speaking with an acquaintance, who was not there.

My imaginary conversation was with my friend, Steve Cole, with whom I had served in the Navy. In my fantasy, he had stayed in the Navy and had served time in Annapolis. In reality, he had gotten out the same time I did. He was pointing out various houses along the route, telling me which Admiral had retired there. He even asked if I would like to stop and have coffee with one. This went on until I was snapped back into total reluctant reality but one extremely close encounter with a car, and the sound of Jacob yelling for me to "GO STRAIGHT!, accompanied by Adam laying on the horn with three successive honks, reiterating their desire for me to go straight utilizing our established signaling system. "Okay, I got it!" I yelled back. However, one more close encounter with a commuter, and I pulled off to the side, fearing for my life. As Jacob and Adam pulled in beside me, I remember asking Jacob, "Why are they trying to kill me?!" Jacob, seeing the panic and disorientation in my eyes, became worried for the first time.

Alarm bells went off, and Jacob sent the word out to the rest of the crew that we may have a problem. As they raced back to the scene (they had already been preparing for the finish), they told Jacob to put me in the car and tell me to sleep. I was beyond sleep, but I did close my eyes. I could hear familiar voices, as well as several I did not recognize. One was the homeowner whose driveway we were blocking. Another was a race official, asking if I was going to be able to continue. Finally, I heard Maria's reassuring voice.

"He's fine.", she was telling the race official.

"He's been sleeping for 45 minutes now (really only 15), and is just about ready to continue."

To prove my coherence, she asked me, "Marshall, do you know your name?"

"Thanks for the clue.", I thought. "Marshall.", I replied.

"Do you know where you are?", she asked.

I was ready for that one, so I answered, "Racing in RAAM, almost in Annapolis." "Come on", she said "It's time to end this thing. There are people waiting for you at the finish line."
Seemingly satisfied, but still a little worried, the race official gave his approval, and my crew helped me back on to the bike.
With less than 20 miles to go, the crew was even more attentive. So was the race official running interference ahead of us. He wanted us to finish as well. I was the "lantern rouge", the red lantern. Last one on the course! This term stemmed from the practice of having a vehicle follow the last cyclist in a bicycle race, in particular the Tour De France, carrying a red lantern, to designate the back of the race.
Every bit of the attention would be needed, as we were about to enter a dangerous section of

the route leading to time station 53 in the Odenton Shopping Center. In order to get there, we had to negotiate four traffic circle roundabouts, and merge onto an interchange with vehicles moving at sixty plus mph. We made it through the roundabouts, but as we started to merge onto the freeway, there was a red pick up truck coming from our right, intent on beating us on to the freeway, and giving no quarter. We had the right of way, so I foolishly continued, ignoring the age old Naval law of gross tonnage, which dictates that even when one vessel may have the right of way, the larger vessel will fare better in the event of a collision, so the smaller vessel should give way. When he realized that we were not going to stop, he slammed on his brakes. I looked over my right shoulder in time to see a red pick up truck coming at me sideways, as his brakes had locked up. I think Adam would have rammed him with the follow car to protect me if needed, but fortunately, the driver of the pickup got it under control in time. From here, it was an uneventful 4 miles to the shopping center, where I saw the welcome sight of a Starbucks sign! We were now 9.4 miles from the finish, as we took one last short break to enjoy a much needed shot of caffeine.

Although the ceremonial finish is at City Dock in Annapolis, the "official" finish is at the Rams Head Roadhouse, 6 miles short of there. This is where you cross a nondescript line painted on the road, and a lone race official stationed to the side to stop the clock and record your official finish time. In many ways this is better, as it gives you the opportunity to reflect on the accomplishment on a personal level, without all the hoopla of the City Dock scene. The incident with the pick up truck had triggered what was left of my adrenaline, and suddenly everything was clearer than it had been in the last 24 hours. As we made our way the last few miles to the Rams Head Roadhouse, I reflected back upon not only this race, but the two prior unsuccessful attempts. It was as though I was on the outside, looking in at someone else who had just done this. I could not believe that that someone was me.

After triumphantly crossing the finish line, complete with a failed "high five" attempt with the race official as I passed, I remember reflecting on just how unlikely this victory was. Not for me, but for us! On paper, this had "failure" written all over it, yet somehow, we prevailed. Now official finishers, we continued to the mandatory stop at the Shell gas station two miles further down the road. This is where riders and crew wait to be escorted across the ceremonial finish line at City Dock. The collective relief was palpable as we awaited our escort.

We were in shock. Despite all odds, we had managed to pull off the nearly impossible. We had crashed a car before the race even started, losing a crew member in the process, gotten our final crew member the day before the start, taken a huge gamble with the Hail Mary rest break in Ohio, lost two crew members near the end, ridden practically non-stop for 50 hours at the end of a 3100 mile long race, and narrowly avoided a collision with a pick up truck near the very end. As the adrenaline wore off, we started to come down from our emotional high. The results were varied. Ryan laid down on the sidewalk, and was instantly sound asleep. I laid down also, but my mind was racing too fast to allow sleep to come. Perhaps I was afraid that if I fell asleep, I would never wake up. Jacob and Adam were still busy, getting my spare bike ready for my son, Jesse, to ride with me across the finish line.

Finally, the escort was ready. Jesse and I mounted our bikes, with me grimacing one last time as I eased my weight down on my open sores. Ryan, Jacob, and Adam climbed into the support cars, and off we went. As we drew near the City Dock, those bystanders who knew what was going on, cheered us in, and those who were not aware, stared in disbelief. As we made the last turn, I could see the finishing banner just ahead. I could also see my wife, Madge, and my daughter, Molly, waiting just off to the side. With Jesse riding next to me, I was emotionally overcome, knowing my whole family was there to share this with me. Also there were members of our media crew, who not only documented our efforts for our charity, "3000 Miles to a Cure", but provided encouragement and support along the way, both personally, and by relaying the inspirational comments of those following our race on social media. Lucia was quickly on the scene with her ever present microphone. She had been providing a live feed as we approached the finish, and wanted a few words. Maria, the consummate cheerleader, was now discretely off to the side, with her nephew, Joe, simply applauding. Having completed this race herself, she knew what I was experiencing, and was happy to share it with me vicariously. Rob DeCou was there as well, having finished the race just a few hours earlier, selflessly awaiting my finish to share in an emotional victory hug. He too, had raced for "3000 Miles to a Cure", and even more important than both of us having finished the race, was that between us, we had raised over $40,000 to be used toward research and the eventual cure for brain cancer. Finally, I was then able to share the moment with my family, who had suffered right along with me the entire way, and hoist my long awaited celebratory Stella Artois beer.

It was over.

EPILOGUE

Race Across America was the hardest thing I have ever done. Looking back, I still have a hard time believing it. With a dedicated crew, and determined rider, failure was simply not an option. Even so, it took a great deal of good fortune and support from dozens of others, many of whom we never met, to make this race a success. Perhaps the single most important factor in our victory, was the inspiration we drew from those following the race, and those we met along the way, whose common bond was the shared specter of brain cancer. Without riding in support of this worthy cause, this would have been an exercise in ego. While we chose to subject ourselves to misery, those with brain cancer did not. We could have stopped at any time and been done with our pain. Those with brain cancer, and their loved ones, do not have that option. Hopefully, with the help of "3000 Miles to a Cure", someday this awful disease will be a thing of the past.

The following pictures and comments were put together by our photographer, Bryan Cereijo. It is from a photo essay he composed for submission to a contest, in which he was awarded first place.

Bryan's essay

The Race Across America (RAAM) – the "World's Toughest Race" - is a 3000 miles bicycle race that starts in Oceanside, CA and ends in Annapolis, MD. This year , I was very fortunate to work for "3000 Miles To a Cure", and document one of their cyclists, Marshall Reeves, as he tried to complete RAAM while raising money for brain cancer research.

I'll let my images do most of the talking but I think Marshall summed it up perfectly in his post-race interview: "It's pretty selfish if all you're doing is [racing]. It's a lot of pain, a lot of training, a lot of sacrifice, but it's something you volunteer for. Whereas people who are afflicted by a lot of diseases, in particular brain cancer, they didn't pick that battle, but they're faced with it, and it's just as daunting and devastating as it can be. Far more so than this race...but if you are diagnosed with brain cancer, it's a death sentence. And so I realized I needed to do something worthwhile with this effort or it would just be for naught.

Marshall completed the race in 12 days, 13 hours, and 52 minutes and raised over $20,000 for brain cancer research. You can still donate by visiting the site: "www.3000Milestoacure.com.

In my images, I wanted to show how grueling this race is and how it pushes racers and their crews to their limits. I wanted to show everything that goes into this 3000 mile journey.

Marshall before the start

Marshall Reeves begins his 3000 mile journey in Oceanside, CA on June 14th, 2016. This was his third attempt at completing the Race Across America, also known as the World's Toughest Race. The difference this year, he was racing to raise money for brain cancer research.

There's a lot of climbing in the Race Across America where racers endurance is tested. Marshall climbed the Yarnell Grade, an 1,800 foot climb over seven miles, almost always pedaling off his saddle. Photo taken by Bryan Cereijo on June 15th, 2016.

One of the more challenging parts of the race is the Wolf Creek Pass climb where cyclists have to climb up to 10,857 feet. The steep grade and lack of oxygen at such a high altitude make it difficult to get through. Marshall stands up to pedal through the pass on June 18th, 2016.

Cramps plagued Marshall through the first several days of the race as he tried to get through the desert. The intense heat during the day and the frigid nights did not help the cause. Pictured is crew member Jacob Bouchard quickly massaging Marshall in his RV during a stop on June 15th, 2016.

Crew member Ryan Jean sleeps in one of the follow vehicles as crew members Tyler Jandreau and Joseph Joseph wait for Marshall to arrive for a quick stop on June 21st, 2016. Marshall's crew consisted of only 6 people who had to alternate shifts while Marshall was on the bike for more than 20 hours a day.

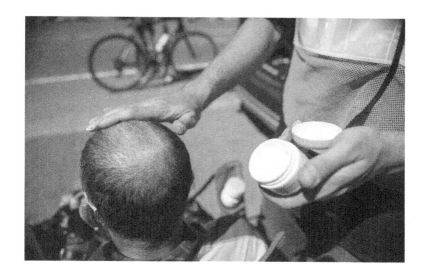

Crew member Tyler Jandreau applies zinc oxide cream to Marshall's head to prevent sunburn during the day ride on June 18th, 2016.

Marshall Reeves passes through Monument Valley in Arizona on June 17th, 2016 as he makes his way to Utah.

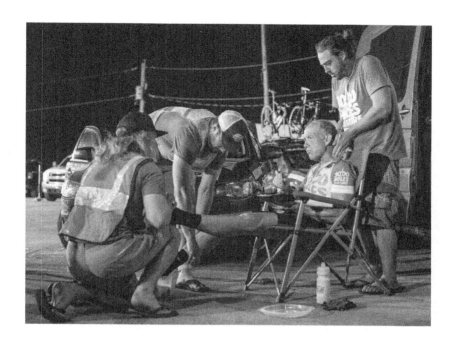

From left to right, crew members Ryan Jean, Tyler Jandreau, and Jesse Reeves massage Marshall as he eats to get him ready for a full night of riding. Marshall had little time to stop as he was trying to make it to the Mississippi River time cutoff. Photo taken on June 22nd, 2016.

Marshall Reeves smiles before heading out for another full night of riding on June 23rd, 2016. By this point, he was 9 days in and had pedaled almost 2,000 miles.

Marshall Reeves passes the Mississippi River bridge on the night of June 23rd, 2016, making the time cutoff. For many racers just getting to this point is a huge accomplishment because it represents completing two-thirds of the race.

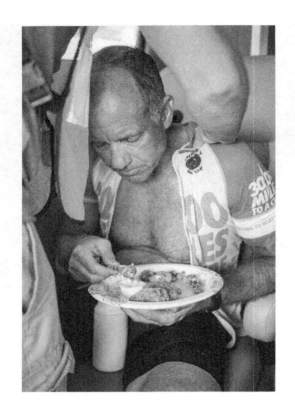

Marshall eats KFC wings his crew got for him, as Jacob Bouchard massages his neck. Marshall still has several all night rides ahead of him.

Marshall Reeves clears a rolling hill in West Virginia on June 25th, 2016. The last stages of the race are difficult because cyclists are plagued with muscle aches and fatigue. Marshall finished the race on June 26th, 2016 with a time of 12 days, 13 hours, and 52 minutes.

And there is is...After going through the thousands of frames, countless re-edits, and advice from peers, those were the 12 I selected and put together to show what Race Across America is and what it takes from an individual to complete. However, there are a few other images that did not make the story that I would love to share because I do think they are valuable:

Maria, encouraging Marshall up Wolf Creek Pass.

Desert beauty (the terrain)

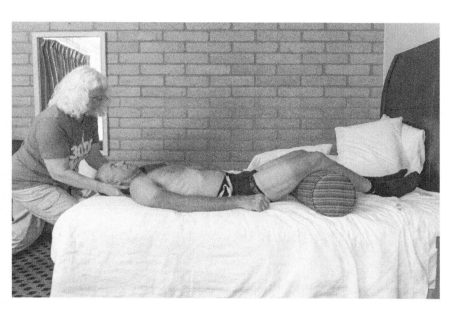

Quick massage

Hours of sheer boredom, punctuated my moments of stark terror

Much of the race was a blur too.

Heading out for another session. The second pair of inside out shorts was to add padding to help with the saddle sores.

(the two photos on the next pages are not from Bryan's essay)

The finish at last!

The crew at the finish (minus Joseph Joseph and Tyler Jandreau)

Made in the USA
Coppell, TX
12 April 2022